Release your inner
HEALING POWER

Release your inner
HEALING POWER

Tom Johanson

Bishopsgate Press Ltd.
37 Union Street, London SE1 1SE

British Library Cataloguing in Publication Data

Johanson, Tom
   Release your inner healing power.
   1. Spiritual healing
   I. Title
   615.8′52   BT732.5

   ISBN 0-900873-89-2
   ISBN 0-900873-90-6 Pbk.

All enquiries and requests relevant to this title should be sent to the publisher, Bishopsgate Press Ltd., 37 Union Street, London, SE1 1SE

Printed in Great Britain by
Whitstable Litho Ltd., Whitstable, Kent

CONTENTS

INTRODUCTION

The title of this book should not be mis-read as to lead the reader to the belief that contact healing by a spiritual healer is unnecessary. Nothing could be further from the truth. But it is a sincere and, I hope, a practical guide for those who suffer illnesses and who wish to understand something of the **inner** causes from which their physical or mental problems originate. As will be explained later these inequalities are **JUST**, not accidental, and the outworking of a Law of Love.

It is also my humble hope that by considering and applying the knowledge put before them they may assist themselves in their own healing. In the first chapter I have dealt in some detail with the **nature of man**, the **nature of disease** and the belief in the **pre-existence of the human soul**. Without first establishing logical grounds for the belief in the **pre-existence** of the soul there are no other possible or logical grounds why new-born children come into this world handicapped with brain tumours, deformed bodies and numerous other physical and mental impediments when **no visible cause** is evident. A burden which many carry throughout their entire life-time. These unfortunate victims start life with a severe handicap whilst others live a life of comparative ease and comfort.

In introducing the ancient doctrines of pre-existence and re-birth some of my readers may react with some measure of emotional interest, curiosity or even antagonism as if some strange foreign faith was attempting to destroy their long cherished beliefs. In my attempt to explain the **gross inequalities** of life, and there are many of them, I must either accept that there is a true, immutable plan of the philosophy of life in which **all** souls are given the same opportunities to progress to a better state of spiritual enlightenment by a just, good and all-loving God, or that God is capable of creating something which any ordinary, decent person would do all in his power to prevent or mitigate. It is our duty, therefore, to consider and courageously examine these ancient doctrines to see if they reveal to us new tracts of truth, important purposes and necessary experiences which, up till now, have remained dark and mysterious.

The doctrines of pre-existence and re-birth have far too long a history to be conveniently pushed aside or ignored. They were first heard among the ancient sages of India after which they found a permanent place in Hinduism and Buddhist philosophy. They were taught by the earliest Greek philosophers, by the Druids of Gaul and in more recent times proclaimed by Goethe, Swedenborg, Lavater, Ibsen and Maeterlinck to mention but a few. In any attempt to formulate a definite plan of life and to see meaning and purpose in the innumerable inequalities these ancient concepts cannot be ignored.

Cicero proclaimed, "Certainly, there appear to be inequalities, but in the light of an assured spiritual future there is justice also".

The reader will also have noticed that we have given much space to the doctrine of Cause and Effect law which declares that man is responsible for **all** acts which generate within his mind. If the genuine student makes a thoughtful study of this living and intelligent law he will soon realise essential principles which prove that man is not only responsible for his own suffering but possesses the power to end his suffering.

He will also realise, as he progresses through the book, that there **is** justice and love in **all** states of inequality – even those seen with the new-born child. More important, I hope he will reach the understanding that man punishes himself **through** his sins and ignorance and not **for** them. Maladies are not only the results of events which have their **cause** in a previous existence but many problems are presently operative because the **cause** was planted a number of minutes, hours, days or just weeks ago. The **effect** (cause must produce an effect) can be experienced within minutes, hours, days or weeks. The law of cause and effect states that if a man commits an act which is motivated by selfishness, greed or hate, which are bad thoughts or causes, pain will surely follow. Just as the wheels follow the feet of he who pulls the carriage, illness and disease may be the effects of bad thoughts.

The problem of human sickness remains a formidable one in spite of the great advance of scientific knowledge that has been achieved in this atomic age. I think it would not be unduly unfair to say that in many areas of human ailments there is a marked failure of modern medical science to produce satisfactory results. The main reason for this is that orthodox methods are administering to **effects** and ignore the **causes**. For too long medical scientists, physicians and psychiatrists have been hypnotised by the disease's physical manifestations whilst the **real** cause has remained deeply hidden in the mind. Disease will never be cured or completely eradicated by materialistic methods because disease is, in truth, the result of conflict between soul and mind. It is only a few years ago that many doctors would have ridiculed the idea of a psychosomatic ailment, in which physical manifestations appear, being due to emotional or mental factors.

However, in chapter 2. I deal in some detail with ailments which though producing painful physical symptoms do not have their origin in the material body. They are products of the mind – a disharmonious mind. Therefore, as you are the only one who has total control of the mind you already have within you the power to correct the disharmony.

I firmly believe I am correct in seeking to establish grounds for the belief in the doctrines of pre-existence and re-birth. Without the establishment of such grounds the hypothesis that there are **no** inequalities in life and that newly-born deformed and diseased children are **not** an accident of birth (but the result of causes created by that soul in a **previous** existence) is not only seriously weakened, but all other possible logical grounds are eliminated. The only other alternative is to assume that what we experience arises from some unknown, uncontrollable power outside ourselves which is simply making a 'game-of-chance' of human life and its destiny. Many of the world's greatest spiritual teachers take their stand on the side of the law of pre-existence (cause and effect), and state that all inequalities in life, including birth and childhood, are the consequences of **prior causes**. Such a viewpoint is the only acceptable one which establishes the logical assurance that we live in a **just** world presided over by a good, all-loving God. It also removes the foolish supposition that God creates certain newly-born souls and places them in positions of comfort and plenty whilst others are made to experience situations of ugliness, squalor, pain and deprivation.

To the reader of this book, who, I presume, is keenly interested in the practice of self-healing, I must point out that much space is given to the inconsequential behaviour of the mind.

This behaviour is primarily the cause of many minor and serious physical disturbances resulting from sudden and sustained alterations in the emotional states. Three of the most fundamental steps towards self-healing are mental discipline, self-observation and the ability to relax at will. To guide the reader towards these achievements I have inserted chapters dealing with the practices of absent, or distant, healing, contact healing, mind relaxation, simple meditation techniques and relatively short descriptions of self-observation and the technique of prayer. The essential purpose of these exercises is to discipline the ever restless mind and introduce a state of 'active-contemplation'. At first these exercises will prove difficult to master because for so long we have lived with an 'impulsive' mind. The mind has never really been under the conscious control of the will and consequently has become as a spoilt child – it has become an inefficient instrument. For most of our life we have done very little 'controlled' thinking and as a result most of our mental states have become highly coloured by distorted emotions. We have never seriously attempted to evaluate the cause of these emotions but always accepted them without question and as a reality. In truth, the mind has developed the characteristics of a grasshopper impulsively leaping from one place to another.

In introducing the practices of absent and contact healing we are following the commands of the world's spiritual teachers, 'As you give, so shall you receive tenfold'. Or, 'Whatsoever a man sows that shall he also reap'. In Oriental philosophy this is the law of cause and effect. Whatever a person does whether it be a kind physical act or a loving thought, somewhere, sometime that act of love and kindness will return to him with added interest. So, in a roundabout but positive way he will receive great benefit. I must emphasise, however, that this is not a question of receiving a reward, it is the inevitable consequence of an inexorable law of spiritual justice which connects all souls and other living things.

Tom Johanson

CHAPTER ONE

FOR EVERY DISEASE THERE
IS A NATURAL CURE

(Hippocrates)

"The cure of a part should not be attempted without treatment of the whole. No attempt should be made to cure the body without the soul and, if the head and the body are to be made healthy, you must begin by curing the mind. That is the first thing. Let no one persuade you to cure the head until he has given you his soul to be cured. For this is the great error of our day in the treatment of the human body, that physicians first separate the soul from the body". Plato, Republic : 380 BC.

Prior to the birth of Plato disease and illness were considered by many to be the vengeance of angry gods wreaked upon those people who had offended them. Others blamed their illness on the unfavourable influence of the stars which were in the wrong position. Plato was among the first of the great philosophers to reject these superstitious theories. Hippocrates, born 460 BC., was believed to be the first physician to search deeper for more natural causes of disease and so he established the technique of examining and observing the **life-style** and **habits** of sick people. Finally he came to the conclusion that **unnatural,** disharmonious living habits and mental disturbances were the cause of most illnesses and diseases. He was the first to teach, "To every disease there is a natural cause, and for every disease a natural remedy". Hippocrates, an outstanding authority on herbs and diets, devoted much of his life to dispensing natural remedies.

During the time of Plato the whole concept of medical analysis changed and turned away from the beliefs of Hippocrates. Medical techniques never recovered from this departure. Physicians and their students began to concentrate

13

almost totally upon the body and its parts because they were convinced that all diseases and illnesses began **within** the material parts. Modern medical science is still based upon this ancient concept that the "whole" is the total of all its component parts. Many scientists and physicians believe that it is only necessary to analyse and understand the working of each component part – the organ and the cell – to gain complete knowledge of the whole (body). Such a narrow-minded and materialistic view reduces the body to nothing more than a machine without soul, mind or spirit.

It was this new concept of medical analysis and the physician's total pre-occupation with organs, bones, muscles and tissue that led to Plato's condemnation of the new system, the quotation which begins this chapter. These methods of medical diagnosis are still basically the same today except that the techniques have become increasingly more complicated and expensive.

Scientists are not at all concerned with giving a serious thought to spiritual forces or recognising a vital spiritual plan of life. They believe the role of the soul and spirit has no part to play in our health, or lack of it. Their only consideration and concentration is collecting codified data of material parts. The world is in danger of becoming entirely anthropomorphic; governed, ruled, judged and administered to by physicists, micro-physicists, biologists and physiological chemists, to mention a few. Each researcher contributes principles derived from his own particular field which frequently do not apply to other fields when, in fact, they should. Unperturbed, each carries on with his own line continuing to disclose fresh discoveries, but, ironically, with each new discovery they reveal more new problems.

In spite of the continual disclosure of new problems the belief of the researcher is never questioned or weakened at all. He still believes he is making progress. The scientist remains totally unaware that he is working in a **quantitative** field. Quantitative science has always failed and will continue to fail to answer **all** questions about our **whole** self which is **material, spirit, mind** and **soul.** That this is the total reason for the failure of modern medical science was first realised by Hippocrates and Plato. The researchers are examining **effects** and ignoring the **causes**. All our endeavours must be directed towards healing the **whole**, but to have any understanding of healing the whole we must first concentrate upon the inner **cause** of disease. Before we can do that we must understand the **nature** of man and the **purpose** of man's pilgrimage through life.

One of the greatest tragedies which has arisen from the advancement of medical knowledge is that it has infused people's minds with its awesome power and infallibility. Any suggestion that they are not only responsible for the maintenance of their own health, but must be concerned and intimately involved in **their own** healing is ridiculed. Unfortunately, they dismiss their illness or disease as an event to which they have contributed nothing – it was an accident! The consequences are that they believe it is the duty of **someone else,** for example the surgeon, the doctor or chemist to put matters right. The idea that their sickness was in no way an accident but a disharmony for which they alone were responsible is regarded with total disbelief and resentment. It was Pythagoras who said, "There are no disharmonies there is only ignorance". To receive any understanding of disease we must first understand the **cause** of disease.

But we begin by attempting to understand man – the **whole** man. He is more, much more than a physical body. Above the physical system, but closely integrated with it, exists a variety of finer bodies, or energy levels. First, forming an intimate link between the physical body and lower mind, or earth mind, is a field of consciously-activated energy. Closely associated with this field is the emotional and intellectual consciousness. Each of the **lower** levels is intimately associated with, and responsible for, physical and mental action **within** and **reaction** to events on the **outside**. Experimentation with and observation of "introduced" disturbances to the physical-emotional-intellectual energy levels have revealed significant alterations in the physical body. In other words, where there was normally a harmonious interplay between the lower energy levels any introduced state of "imbalance" would manifest as a psychosomatic or physical-psychic disturbance. The experiment clearly indicated that the physical-emotional-intellectual levels of mind can disrupt the normal functions of the mind and eventually manifest as a physical disturbance or disease.

The most common mental disturbances we experience are fear, anger, hate, embarrassment, frustration, anxiety, lust, resentment, panic and shock. But, conversely, the body through accidental injury, disease, misuse, neglect, fatigue and over-strain can create a variety of mental disturbances which if prolonged will create a "repeat" and react upon the physical system. Every human being is endowed with a natural "in-built" system of self-healing, but man's obsession with the physical body and his "conditioned" materialistic approach to solving its problems plus his failure to recognise the "whole" has seriously limited the true concept of his **real** self and so the body's natural and vital self-healing system becomes inhibited.

The physical-emotional-intellectual levels enable man to communicate in every way with the outer sensual world and in return receive the experiences he desires and also the knowledge. In addition to these "lower" levels he also exists on a psychical and an infinite variety of spiritual levels of consciousness. Through these higher levels he receives such phenomena as the **intuitive** perception of the emotions and feelings of others. It is through this level that he is able to receive wisdom – the knowledge of himself – and become conscious of higher "values" of spiritual significance such as Love, Truth, Beauty, Goodness, Compassion and Inspirational Thought. This **higher** mind can, and does, throw much light upon the function of the lower minds and can substantially "explain", or convey, the exact nature of the lower. Because the higher order will, in time, illuminate and provide "understanding" of the lower this provides the knowledge and means for the soul's progression. The lower minds cannot tell us what beauty is or why it exists. It cannot explain the source of inspiration. It cannot tell us what love is or the place of its origin. The lower mind can help us to search for truth but it does not know why man is anxious to discover it. The answer to these mysteries lies in the highest levels of our consciousness. The all-important functions of the higher minds are to slowly, painstakingly guide man to eventually realise his **true** self – the SPIRIT. But this will only be achieved through **total** understanding and mastery of the lower self. He must go through a long process of experiencing the **opposite** of every emotion.

Our sensual and intellectual self is slowly, continuously being conditioned by its environment and the process of "conditioning" only operates **below** the spiritual levels. The conditioning is fraught with trials and painful experiences, sometimes taking the form of anger, depression, disappointment, anxiety, frustration and illness. The process is, in a way, a merciful provision because it eventually and ironically achieves a harmonious relationship between the man and his environment. He will realise, in the end, that **all** progress really depends upon the initial sensual desire which was responsible for the disharmony. For example, the consequences of overeating, or not eating, over-drinking, smoking etc., dramatically demonstrate the dangers of man's ignorance of the powers his lower senses have over him. However uncomfortable the process may be we must accept and realise that every weakness, which will sooner or later, be exploited is a necessary means available to us to progress. We are born into this earth and are conditioned by it on all levels, physical, emotional and intellectual, but I **know** that our feet are set on an intelligible pilgrimage, and that there is divine love at the heart of **all** things and experiences. However, the real value of experiencing the impermanent and the perishable lies not at all in what it achieves on the physical plane. Its value lies in the **understanding,** the awareness, the experience which is supplanted within the soul. What happens to these acts of ignorance which man has performed? Time sweeps them away, but the **knowing** – the memory of the **nature** of the experience is an imperishable thing, therefore something of the greatest value.

All "things" offer experiences; bodies, sensations, emotions, desires which are impermanent and perishable but the vital root of all suffering lies in **desire** – an emotional attachment to "things" which is destined to pass away. The basic philosophy of the great spiritual masters was to show men how to escape from the outer, the perishable and impermanent way of life to the inner world in which all things are infinite and permanent.

Every action is the outworking, on an earth level, of our deeper selves, and the nature of the action is determined by the nature or quality of our desire. We alone make the decision whether to act selfishly through greed, anger, jealousy, fear, hatred or desire for power and fame. This is attachment to the perishable and limited, therefore, as is the conscious expression so the resultant consequences will be of the **same** nature. It is therefore important to realise that the effect of desire and action on the outside world is a two-way process; that whilst we are attempting to satisfy the baser level of mind these baser levels will ultimately reflect their quality upon the body and the mental states. This means that not only is the mind capable of disorganising the normal operation of the physical body, for example, high blood pressures, ulcers, indigestion, hyperthyroidism and other physical diseases, but the body is capable of creating certain mental disorders which, in turn, react upon the body. All these creations, whether mental states, body functions or objective entities reflect the quality or level of mind manifesting. Just as we have described how the mind is capable of producing harmony, disharmony, beauty or ugliness in manipulative materials so the same effects can be created in the human body which is, after all, a material object.

The act of healing, whether it be spiritual, orthodox or self-healing, if it is to be successful, is to restore the state of mental harmony. The inner self-healing system is activated when the sick person calmly and courageously recognises those constant, disturbing aspects and emotions within his daily life which unconsciously and automatically create inner imbalances. The main reason why the potential self-healer fails every time to experience **permanent** relief is because he automatically and consciously focuses his remedies upon the **effects** and ignores the **cause**.

The cause is the inner mental disturbance which, in time, produces physical effects. The same charges can be laid at the feet of medical scientists who, ever since the days of Plato, have failed to recognise the **real nature** of disease because of their obsession with materialism. For centuries disease has continued and extended its ravages because few, very few, have thought to attack it at its origin.

I willingly concede that it is extremely difficult for a physician, who has spent many years in a medical college concentrating upon the complex and myriad functions of the body's numerous organs, to believe and understand how anything of an abstract nature, such as anger, frustration, hate, greed, jealousy and unremitting fear can have a physical and functional effect upon a physical organ. No more than he can understand that calmness, love, tranquillity, compassion and happiness can correct it. So long as the self-healer and the medical men remain limited in their concept of the **whole** man, disease will always continue to be one step ahead of them. The entire medical world desperately needs a **wider concept of the nature of man.** Until that time doctors will simply carry on "patching-up" the body and, often, burying the cause without knowing **why** there was no effect. Of course, everyone knows of someone who was ill and who was apparently cured by orthodox methods. The vital question is, how **many** times has that person been "cured" of various problems? It would be unusual and unexpected for that person to remain perfectly healthy for the rest of their life. This is because the underlying cause will, from time to time, produce a variety of effects which will **temporarily** respond to material treatment until the real cause has been removed. As we shall see later in this book, no material effort, no matter how sophisticated or scientifically advanced, if applied solely to the body will achieve more than superficial relief.

Because the cause remains and is still operative. At any time it can, and it will, demonstrate its powers in a variety of disturbing forms. The dangers inherent in this modern and generally accepted approach to treatment of illnesses is that as long as the true cause remains concealed from the patient, and unknown to the doctors, the strength of the operative cause may continue to develop. It is not my wish, with regard to this statement, to unduly alarm the reader concerning the possibility, or impossibility, of eradicating an illness, but if they will carefully consider the viewpoints already given they will soon realise that **all** illnesses are directly the result of prevailing disharmonies between **their** mind and soul. In which case they, themselves, already possess the necessary powers to nullify the disturbing forces. Spiritual and mental powers alone are the only forces which can totally eradicate disease. Material medicines will never achieve this result. They can only achieve a temporary effect.

Never since the early days of Hippocrates and Plato has any ancient or modern physician attempted to challenge the firmly established and universally accepted practices of modern medicine. There are, however, two exceptions. The first was Hahnemann, the legendary German physician. He was one of the first in his time to realise the Divine entity which resides within man's soul – the infinite power of love and healing which is man's natural heritage. Like the great Hippocrates before him he instinctively sought to find the answers to illnesses by studying mental attitudes and reactions to certain environments. Intuitively, he felt that the answers to man's physical and mental problems could be found in Nature's resources. Tirelessly, as did Hippocrates, he sought and experimented with herbs of the countryside and finally founded the science of homeopathy.

As Hippocrates became known as the Father of Medicine so Hahnemann is recognised as the Father or Homeopathy. The other exception is to be found as long ago as 500 years B.C. Some Buddhist physician-monks working in the the temples of ancient India advanced the art of self healing and spiritual healing to such a degree of perfection that they were able to abolish surgery completely in spite of the fact that their particular surgical techniques were superior to those of today.

Working under the influence of Buddhist philosophy, they realised the absolute certainty of the divinity in man, the real nature of illness and that all diseases originated in a plane of consciousness beyond the physical.

The reader should pause for a moment at this point and realise that these same powers are, as with the Buddhist physicians, already with him. He must learn to reach within himself and much of his misery can be alleviated. The modern world is still firmly within the grip of materialism and the voices of scientific practitioners still rise loudly above those few who **know** the nature of materialism, the true nature of man which is not now, nor ever will be material.

CHAPTER TWO

THERE IS NO DISEASE, ONLY IGNORANCE

(Pythagoras)

Our present system of living, when we consider it, is clearly a state of association of mind with a material world. The association with a world of "objects" begins in childhood from the earliest awareness of self. This initial self-awareness, or simple-consciousness, continues to develop right up to and through adulthood. With the development of the "self" instinct commences a growing awareness of the **need** for the things of the world. This process of expanding self-awareness is insidiously affected by a rising sense of insecurity which is naturally linked with the growth of the instinct of self-preservation. At the end of this natural, but necessary, cycle the subject becomes more and more dependent upon the world and its objects. The world, which he believes is there to minister to him, is his only means of achieving security, comfort, power and eliminating the two persisting fears which threaten his existence. The first of these is the fear of not achieving that which he desires most, and the other is the fear of losing the objects or power he already possesses. These fears, created by emotions and attitudes which were wholly self-centred, are inevitably affected by conflict, struggle, greed, jealousy, suspicion and cunning. Insatiable desires provide the driving force and all outside resistance to further possession is considered a danger and a menace to ambitions and his very existence and must, therefore be fought and eliminated. During this phase there is little love, only disharmony and a discordant mind which, at a later time, reveals that this state of mind is not only capable of disrupting the normal operating of the body, but the over-stressed body is capable of triggering off certain mental states.

Many serious physical disruptions resulting directly from persistent changes in the emotional and physical states have been clinically proven. The professional rate of cancer, ulcerated stomachs, cardiovascular diseases, hypertension, alcoholism, drug addiction and suicide is tragic evidence of this.

Health is not only a condition of balance between mind and soul (which together with the physical make up the WHOLE of man) but between the ego-man and his ambitions, hopes, desires, fears, employment and environment. Plato goes even further than this and includes all the environmental sub-conscious memories from former incarnations. Many ask the question, "If there is a God and man is essentially and eternally an indivisible part of Him, what is the object and purpose of inflicting disease, mental disharmony, limitation and hindrance upon His subjects?" We have only to look to creations of nature to find positive clues to this baffling question. The first thing we witness is the natural process of constant change. The seed is transformed into a flower and then back to the seed again to repeat the cycle. Trees produce leaves only to shed them, but are again replaced by new ones. Day gives way to night, winter to summer. The small acorn becomes a giant oak. A fertilised ovum produces a human child and the animal. Youth matures into manhood. Change is the manifestation of a **dynamic** life force continuously producing new forms of life. As nature in all its forms is perfect organisation it cannot therefore be a **static** force. In all varieties of human, animal and vegetable there is first embryonic form. Nature, therefore, apart from creating the embryonic **physical** man also creates embryonic **spiritual** beings (simple consciousness).

As a child matures and gradually acquires the wisdom of manhood through the painful processes of experience, so the embryonic consciousness of man matures through limitation and suffering. In this way he eventually comes to **know** his eternal-self. How can he perceive the significance of light if he does not at first experience, or suffer, darkness? How can he come to know peace if he does not experience pain? How can he realise the significance of immortality if he does not experience

24

mortality? How can he recognise reality (spirit) if he does not suffer illusion (material)? How would he know the power of wisdom, of the infinite, if he does not know ignorance or limitation? To achieve realisation of one's true, unlimited self requires first, a long, slow descent into matter – the school of darkness, illusion and limitation – and then a long, slow **ascent** from which the truth of one's immortal, infinite state is gradually uncovered.

It is hoped that at this stage it is becoming apparent to the reader that though many experiences in life (including disease, deformity and all other mental and physical impediments –) appear to be cruel, meaningless and sometimes even evil they are also beneficent and, in reality, for our own good. It is also hoped, through the services of this book, that they will be guided to recognise the nature of their painful transgressions against the natural laws. Furthermore, that if the knowledge is acted upon in the correct way it may lead the reader to recognise and remove the essential **causes** so leave him happier and healthier than before.

Before we can embark upon a plan to heal ourselves we must first become familiar with certain basic principles which potentially contribute towards the development of diseases and illnesses. The first of these is the ego-self (or surface mind), that part which ordinary (unenlightened) people **believe** themselves to be and with which they positively associate themselves. This is the impermanent self, – that level of consciousness on which we experience the disturbing clash of opposites both good and bad, hate and love, happiness and misery, success and failure, generosity and greed, peace and pain or fear. The ego-self is also known as the level of primary ignorance because as long as we keep it in being we remain totally ignorant of our true nature. Cravings and desires for the sensual things of the world are constant expressions of the ego's search for happiness and security, but as the objects are impermanent the happiness and security experienced is limited and soon fades away. This increases the sense of insecurity, therefore, the fear and dissatisfaction of life. For a time the ego-self refuses to accept the state of impermanence (illusion) of the desire-object and continues to search on the **outside** for **inner** happiness. Although the material world is a world of **appearance** only and the experiences it offers are limited, and for a time we are its prisoner (attached by desires and cravings) we cannot ignore that it **is** there not by accident, but because of divine reason. Therefore, there is a divine reason for us being drawn to it and why we are its prisoner. Thus it is our prime duty to find out why. The second principle is that man has a soul which is the vehicle for every level of consciousness from the low material levels to the absolute state of divine consciousness – which the Indian mystics refer to as **Samadhi**.

Our normal or earthly level of conscious living is experienced first on the lower levels and this applies to every soul. It is of great importance that the reader should strive with all the power of concentrated thought to fully understand the necessity for the existence of these lower levels and how our greatest happiness and assured progress is born of the fact that we experience these harsh, low-level actions and elements to guide and direct us.

The would-be **self-healer** must fully accept this life of physical action and reaction in a world of physical appearance. In spite of its hardness and difficulties it gathers for us potentially important knowledge, knowledge concerning the nature of the ego-self. Admittedly, this knowledge of itself cannot ascend to the higher spiritual levels, but the actions committed on the physical plane together with the inevitable re-actions bring about the outworking and development of the lower-self. All of these actions are the conscious expression of the nature, or the reflection of the **quality**, of consciousness we are projecting onto the physical world. If there are elements of greed, hate, anger or sensual desire the effects which ultimately and inevitably return to us are like mirrors vividly and dynamically revealing the exact and true nature of our actions. The basic incentive to all action is the search for security and happiness and the only difference between the actions of the spiritually wise person and the spiritually ignorant is that the former is searching by way of spiritual motives in which case the happiness gained will be real and without limit. The latter person is searching with materialistic motives. In this case he will suffer the "clash" of opposites; success and failure, happiness and misery, fulfillment and frustration, love and hate, health and disease.

The importance of the law of opposites regarding the education of the soul is clearly stated in W. MacNeile Dixon's book, **The Human Situation,** "This clash of opposites may have brought it about that we have a universe at all, and that we, its offspring, are in being, that from the dark soil of conflict (earth life) creation sprang. But for these oppositions in nature and human life "the world-wide warfare of the eternal two" nothing would have taken place, all would be sunk in a motiveless, motionless stagnation". The soul **knows** what environment and experiences will be best to allow us to eventually overcome the baser and painful elements of life. Every experience attracted to the soul must be looked upon as a succession of **spiritual** opportunities. Let us now summarise the second principle which simply states that we are deliberately placed in the physical world for the express purpose of gaining all the knowledge and experience which can be achieved only through the limitations of the earth; of developing spiritual knowledge concerning our true self through the process of experiencing and suffering all things which are not **real** or permanent. Next follows perhaps the greatest principle of all which was recognised and forcefully advocated long ago by the great philosopher and physician, Hippocrates. It was that as long as the soul and the mind are in harmony all will remain peaceful, happy and healthy. The soul and mind when in harmony walk a pathway which is not entangled in the world of action nor is it troubled by desire. No matter what your station in life, beggar-man or king, rich man or poor man, intellectual or moron every soul contains the necessary lessons and experiences which will involve sickness and unhappiness, but every lesson can, and will, be understood.

At the end stands the spiritual-man – the spiritually wise man

27

whose vehicle of expression which has for so long conveyed the slave of desire is finally left behind at the entrance to the pathway. But it must be clearly understood that this freedom is something which has to be fought for, suffered and won by the way already described. Vital amongst the many fundamental exercises for the development of inner-unity, and recovery of health, is correct and concentrated mind discipline which will be dealt with later. Unfortunately, but necessarily, recognition of the correct pathway is not easily accomplished. Again and again, after searching to find the doorway which will lead to freedom it repeatedly eludes the searcher. This is because the blindness is in the **mind** and **soul** and not in the eyes.

The next task is to still the troublesome, impulsive mind. Through the following sustained practice eventually a higher level of mind slowly awakens with the result profound insights and intuitive knowledge become available to subdue inner conflict. To begin with think of the lower abdomen as an area filled with a bright light. Imagine the warmth and tranquillity. Also imagine that many rays of light are striking out in all directions reaching every part of the body from tips of toes to the head. In your imagination this becomes a reality. You actually create this phenomenon because the Absolute Cause – the Infinite Spirit – is within every soul in all its entirety. We are not **part** of God, but the **whole** of God. Now think of these rays not only as an inseparable part of the Infinite Spirit of higher mind, but as a **thought** of God shining upon and nourishing each part it strikes.

Therefore if you have a troubled part concentrate the ray upon it, but concentrate so that you become totally immersed in it. Remember, spirit is light and light is love. The only action which can effectively cut off the light is an injurious thought or action directed against someone, this includes jealousy, anger, envy, hate and fear, etc. All hatred, anger, aggression, physical and mental aggression is direct judgement and condemnation of another. So there are two **creative** actions we can take. One, associating ourselves with this inner blazing sun of beneficence and love bringing inner harmony and healing and, two, creating

28

disassociation between the mind and the soul which means conflict and inner darkness that eventually lead to illness and disease. The reader should be reminded that the lower self is an old warrior, tenacious and a master of putting misleading and doubtful thoughts into the mind. The exercise of active contemplation, described above, will achieve very little at first. Through constant, sustained practice the lower-self will slowly come under your control.

Two thousand and five hundred years ago Buddha not only recognised the root of all disease and mental suffering in "desire", i.e., emotional attachment to things which because of their nature must pass away, but he also disclosed that the only way man can escape from the transient, and the suffering it created, was to fully understand the nature of the transient. He also advocated that we should recognise that adverse and difficult circumstances could be a divine opportunity of great spiritual advance to higher levels of consciousness.

In other words, disease in itself could be beneficent as its sole object is to bring vividly to the mind the realisation of the mistakes we are making. The realisation could, and eventually will, intuitively guide us to correct these harmful ways through spiritual and mental efforts. Obviously, there are many people who feel antipathetic to the concept that anti-spiritual thoughts, patterns of desire and the law of cause and effect are the only cause of our suffering. It is unfortunately true that the average thoughtful Western man has given very little thought to these deeper matters. Nevertheless, only a complete fool would blockishly sweep aside the numerous ancient scriptures which have not only formulated an acceptable philosophy of life and given logical reasons for man's difficult pilgrimage through life, but have commended themselves to a legion of seers, sages, prophets, masters and advanced spiritual teachers. If the general concept of man is physical/mind/soul then we are compelled by the affirmations of the world's mystics and seers to accept that man exists on different levels and that each level is rooted in higher ones. All mystics claim to have had experiences in these higher levels but say its nature is incommunicable in words. Nevertheless, they are unanimously united in the knowledge they have brought back concerning the nature of man, the nature of the world and the great benefit the experiences bestow upon us. Radhakrishnan, a soul of the highest spiritual order, provides us with important clues when he expressed himself in this way:

"The oldest wisdom in the world tells us that we can consciously unite with the divine whilst in the body, because for this man was really born. If he misses his destiny nature is not in a hurry; she will catch him up one day and compel him to fulfill her secret purpose".

Nature's secret purpose is, it is clear, that we are destined to be united with our many levels of consciousness. As we contemplate Radhakrishnan's statement we are driven to ask ourselves the following questions; How can man miss his destiny and how will nature catch up with him someday? As has already been said, obviously man's destiny is to link up with his higher levels of consciousness and the only way in which he can miss his destiny is to be too preoccupied with things on the lower levels of consciousness. If the higher levels (divinity) are reality then man must be occupying himself with the transient – that which is illusory. The second question; How does nature **compel** him to fulfill her secret purpose? The answer lies in our ego-mind, that centre of ourselves which sustains a craving for the illusory objects with which we falsely identify ourselves. The ego-self, when in command, constantly "screens" the real self by its dominance. One of the most concise summaries of the whole process of nature's secret purpose is again given by *Radhakrishnan. "If we think that our nature is limited by the little wave of our being which is our conscious waking self, we are ignorant of our true being. The relation of our life to a larger spiritual world betrays itself even in the waking consciousness through our intellectual ideals, our moral aspirations, our craving for beauty and our longing for perfection. Behind our conscious self (earthly) is our secret being without which the

*Radhakrishnan. From Eastern Religions and Western Thought.

superficial consciousness cannot exist or act. Consciousness in us is partly manifest and partly hidden (secret). We can enlarge the waking part of it by bringing into play ranges of our being which are not hidden. It is our duty to become aware of ourselves as spiritual beings, instead of falsely identifying ourselves with the body, life (earth) or mind".

Naturally, most people are completely ignorant of the reasons for their illnesses and other distressing incidents which appear to be cruel, accidental and without reason. Nevertheless, the deeper part of the soul is fully aware, in fact, suffering the daily array of disharmonious thoughts and harmful habits. But, still, nature remains patient and continues to provide every possible opportunity for us to change our ways before the body's inner natural healing processes break down. Then we suffer pain, discomfort or mental anguish. Pain and suffering are the warning bells of the soul. When they begin to ring, they are indicating that we are committing cardinal sins against the physical, soul and mind. It is impossible for disease to start up by itself. Remember, disease and pain are the **effects** therefore we, ourselves, that is the living consciousness, provide the **cause**. A motor car, for example, may be perfectly sound mechanically, containing sufficient gasoline, but it takes the **consciousness** of the driver behind the controls to make the car become an active component. Every possible action, movement, physical and mental, needs consciousness behind it to allow it to come alive. As has already been said in previous chapters, the quality of the action depends completely upon the quality of the consciousness.

If we continue with the analogy of the car and the driver we may observe identical similarities between the human body and its consciousness (the driver). For example, inserting poor quality gasoline (food and drink) would create a disruptive performance; aggressiveness (disharmonious mind) is the cause of accidents; insufficient maintenance (body, soul and mind hygiene) prepares the way for ultimate breakdown of parts; lack of respect and care (love) not only creates a slow depreciation of image and presentation but attracts other degenerative elements.

31

Therefore, the "driver" who obeys and honours the spiritual dictates of the soul and whose mental and physical activities are in unity is guiding his vehicle safely and surely because of a spiritually developed consciousness, instinct and intuition. Thus we see through these basic principles and their essence that all breakdowns and interruptions can be avoided or cured.

The reader has been reminded in the preceding chapter that disease and illness are the terminal stages of a disharmony lying deep in an inner level of consciousness and to bring about a complete cure we must search for and eliminate the cause. To deal with the outward effects would be a complete waste of effort. Disease, as everyone knows, can manifest as a physical eruption or mental disorder. If it were possible to have within our nature an abundance of love for **all** things and persons we would be incapable of doing ourselves any harm nor would we be capable of doing harm to anyone else because the presence of love would have complete control over the dictates of the soul. Our hands would be incapable of violent action and the mind would project no words of anger, hate or threat, to hurt another. The healthy way of action means discipline by love and understanding on the physical plane. It is a discipline which is not easily acquired, because as long as the ego-mind is in possession it will make things virtually impossible. The way ahead involves renunciation of the desire for sensual objects and a controlled attitude to success and failure. A formidable task indeed but, as Jesus said, "If there was an easier way I would have told you". Nevertheless, every soul must make a start at some time, but nature, though patient, is determined that a start you will **make** – so why not NOW? However, remember, illness and disease are never signs of total failure.

They can be beneficent in that they positively point out to us when we are applying the wrong emotions and actions. By keeping this thought in mind it actually hastens our recovery from inner and outer disturbances. Let us again briefly examine some of the primary causes which are at the centre of mental diseases. Each of the causes or defects are conscious expressions which because of their nature are the absolute opposite to inner

32

unity or mind harmony. This expression is always an act of desire for something of an impermanent nature. It is for this reason that all the great doctrines of spiritual philosophy implore us to seek and act with an understanding of the nature of that which is not permanent. Impermanence offers only disillusionment, frustration and prepares the way for further desire. Therefore the most common diseases of man are created by such impermanent acts as self-love (selfishness), greed, pride, cruelty, insecurity and hate. Each of these actions, if considered carefully, are the direct opposites of unity of soul and mind, and harmony. These are real mental diseases and if sustained, ignored and allowed to develop will almost surely, at a later date, manifest in the body, or the mind, as a serious disturbance.

Let us now consider these mental acts which precipitate in the body and mind as illness:

SELFISHNESS or SELF-LOVE: This act is an **inward** flow of mental energy and is, therefore, a total reversal of spiritual flow which in a healthy person flows outwards. We are putting our personal interests before the welfare and love of all others. This immediately blocks any love interest and blessings which may come to us from others around us. A most injurious, unnatural flow.

GREED: This is the most potent of all desires. It is the desire for power but also reveals a total ignorance of the needs of others. The ego-mind is totally in command and is blind to everything of a spiritual nature. This is a kind of spiritual starvation and like all experiences of starvation it is degenerative. The ego-mind never experiences permanent satisfaction and therefore the act is continuous and eventually debilitating.

PRIDE: This act recognises nothing of humility and as humility is one of the greatest of spiritual gifts there is no unity whatsoever between mind and soul. The ego-mind is very strong and dominant, therefore for a long time no freedom is awarded to spiritual thoughts and motives. The consequences of a plant being deprived of air and sunlight are duplicated within the soul.

CRUELTY: This indicates a total absence of spirituality. No warm thoughts go out to another. There is a complete lack of recognition of the divine power in others. Darkness is the reigning force in which the mind believes that all injurious effects experienced are the fault of other people. This in turn creates other disturbing and damaging thoughts within the mind. Unfortunately, this increases the mind's desire to seek revenge upon others. However, various injurious effects will, ultimately, be experienced by the thinker until the developing inner awareness helps him to realise the truth. Only then will he achieve relief.

INSECURITY: This emotion always develops when there is a total reliance upon the sensual and impermanent objects of the world. Total ignorance of the inner **permanent** self eventually leads them to betray others and, at the same time, betray themselves. Unwittingly, they are denying themselves the security of the reality of the permanent inner self.

HATE: Is the direct opposite of love. Love is the positive, warm, living divine expression of the deeper God-force within. Hate is a total contradiction of the divine plan and a complete denial of the divine spirit within. Actions from such a controlled mind are dark, evil and destructive not only to others, but much more so to the soul within.

IGNORANCE: This indicates the inability of the thinker to recognise anything of a spiritual, wholesome nature. Again and again the law of cause and effect will offer opportunities to lead the thinker to commit acts of spirituality, but many times it fails. However, the law of nature is never-endingly patient. The persistent state of ignorance will lead the thinker to commit many acts which will react in a harmful way. That is, every act will at some time be experienced and the effects will eventually bring about an inner realisation of the destructive nature of the actions. Disease and illness in all these cases are, strange to say, in the long run beneficent.

The point has now been reached where the reader must positively contemplate the many truths, directives and pointers to the **real** meaning and purpose of life; the greatly diversified forms of suffering, much of which is illness and disease. The greatest points of emphasis in this book have been upon (1) **Cause** and (2) Man is **Spirit** and **Material.** All causes are created in the mind which has, seemingly, an inseparable relationship with what we call an "outside-world" and its numerous objects. This level of mind is the mind of the temporal or, impermanent, man. This objective world is the one which man believes is real and permanent with the result he struggles all his life to make it real. What is really happening is that the finite mind is struggling to maintain an unnatural **inward** flow to self. Always he fails never knowing why but continues to suffer frustration, fear and unfulfillment.

The mind of spirit is the only reality and the only source of permanent harmony. The way to spirit-mind, or the **real** man, involves a gradual renunciation of the desires and, therefore, the attachments of the impermanent mind. It is the long way and the difficult way of developing loving attention to all men, all things and all experiences. This one way the **outward** flowing of spirit to mankind is not only as nature wants it but it is nature's secret purpose which one day everyman will embrace. Only then will all things which are impermanent and troublesome fall away. Disease and illness are impermanent states and can only be created by the impermanent mind. The way of renunciation is the only way in which unity between mind and soul can be achieved and sustained. The Bhagavad Gita speaks of this unity in this way:

"He who experiences the unity of life, sees his own self in **all** beings and all beings in his own self, and looks at everything with an impartial eye. He who sees Me in everything and everything in Me, him shall I never foresake, nor shall he lose Me". The reader must make the discovery that he exists on two different levels. Once he realises this the way ahead is clear and firm. The body and the mind **must** be regarded as instruments on different levels of consciousness which lies behind them. Only the real (spirit) self has total freedom but with the materialistic man it gets very little opportunity to exercise it. This because the ego-mind is too strong. This is the source of all disease and the **origin** of all suffering, disharmony and distress. These conditions, it must be stressed again, are impermanent states because their origin lies in an impermanent source.

Love, kindness, tolerance and compassion are the only states of reality. They are not only experiences to encourage renunciation but positive opportunities for spiritual expansion.

It would also be good to keep before the consciousness the fact that every illness or disturbance from which we suffer can serve as an effective guide to help us to discover the **cause** which lies behind our illness. Let us examine a few simple examples. Bring to mind a person who reflects hate. Note how lonely that person is. In almost every case such a person is given to broodiness, violent tempers, easily aroused displays of irritation and impatience. Greed and selfishness rob another person of a great deal of enjoyment. The sufferer is a complete slave to the body's demands and ambitions. This total attachment to the desires for the impermanent things creates insecurity, fear, jealousy, anxiety, suspicion, envy and anger. Very often there develops the desire to dominate those who possess or can provide the objects he needs. The penalties created by this state of mind are often depression, neurosis, ulcers, hypertension, neurasthenia and a host of other psychosomatic illnesses. Mental anguish and physical pain may be the effects of certain acts of cruelty inflicted on someone a long time ago. The mind – the **source** of the cruelty is inflicting **itself** upon the owner. Therefore, the law of cause and effect is **fortunately** providing the sufferer with an opportunity to learn through personal experience the effects of pain. The result will be at some convenient time that the law's "pupil" will be able to identify himself with the pain he witnesses in others. As Krishna said, "Pain is progress, pain is cleansing". So, in time, the sufferer will learn never to deliberately inflict suffering upon others.

Spiritual ignorance always delivers its own particular brand of experience and difficulties. Man desires all objects and ambitions only because of the **experience** it imparts to our senses.

The life of all objects is limited, therefore the experience it transfers to our senses is limited. The spiritually ignorant man refuses to realise this with the result when the life of the article is ended there arises the urgent desire to keep it in being so he replaces the object over and over again. Often this effort is accompanied by fear and anxiety. There is also always present the fear of losing the articles he possesses or the fear of not getting sufficient. And so cumulative fears create the destructive emotions of greed, selfishness, suspicion, jealousy, hate, envy and possessiveness. And so these pernicious desires impose a great stress upon the body's functional system with the result that the heart, lungs, eyes and digestive system are seriously disturbed. It is also clinically recorded that this destructive emotional pattern speeds up the ageing processes of the body.

Arrogance and pride create rigidity of the mental processes which in time are harmful to certain physical organs. These attitudes arouse disturbing reactions from within other persons with whom they come into contact. And, as we have seen so many times, these reactions, in turn, irritate the senses of the first party. This is an example of where the law of cause and effect operates almost immediately. As we survey the pageant of life and the variety of experiences constantly demonstrated in human life we should no longer harbour any doubts about the exactness and necessity for the law of cause and effect. It is indeed a just law. There is no way in which our bodies and our minds can be affected accidentally. The vital purpose of this law is two-fold. First, it allows us to experience the wrongs we have created for ourselves and done to others. Then inexorably and patiently it provides the means to allow us to **know** the exact nature of the wrong.

In other words, we actually suffer the full experiences of the wrong we committed. We are allowed to establish an individualised ego by doing all the selfish things and when we have experienced every lower grade of **descent** we are then helped and encouraged by (the law) every possible, though painful, means to climb up the soul's ascending pathway. This is accomplished as the earlier phases of ignorance, selfishness and evil are discarded. At this point try a simple test of self-analysis.

Bring to mind the many fits of violent temper, irritations, shocks and emotions of panic which have resulted from certain trivial circumstances. Think of the extreme effects these have had on the brain, heart, blood pressure, digestive system and general nervous system, then carefully question yourself about the causes and motives which triggered them off. Was it pride, greed, fear, envy, jealousy, possessiveness, worry, selfishness, a desire for power or recognition? Every one of these damaging impulses were illusionary, impermanent, mere shadows without real substance. Within a few days, weeks or months these disruptive motives, self-centred impulsive responses will have passed out of the mind and been forgotten. However, the damage to the self will remain because the **cause** will still be in existence – the conflict between mind, body and soul – ready to unleash its damaging forces again and again.

Nevertheless, there is no need for total despondency. We are constantly being helped to discover and recognise these forces within. We can, however, speed up our recovery and prevent further outbursts not by fighting and opposing the conflicting forces, but by constantly bringing to mind and sustaining spiritual thoughts and by checking the spontaneous impulsive thought reactions to specific conditions. This may sound too simple and even impossible to the reader.

But nothing is more certain than that the most material and unspiritual of persons will one day become an evolved spiritually-wise being. To achieve anything that is worthwhile there must first be a long, adequate preparation, determination and an abundance of patience. The soul is embarking upon a most crucial journey, a journey which it is destined to complete – a journey to LIFE! Not everyone is capable of running several kilometres at the first attempt, but if they practise a little every day, with patience, with fortitude, the day will come when they will be able to run the distance without effort.

Once again, let us experiment with another simple soul-exercise. First, for several minutes contemplate the fact that the ego-mind is also an impulsive mind. Whenever a difficult or irritating situation arises it immediately, without pausing to think, jumps in, judges and condemns. The thoughtless impulse could have for its motive, greed, jealousy, hate, envy, possessiveness and so on. On the other hand, the spirit-mind, dormant, remains unaffected, calm and patient never judges or condemns. Therefore, our first move during this exercise, when confronted by an irritating situation, is to check the action of the impulsive-mind. Next, ask yourself, "By which mind shall I evaluate this situation"? Impulsive anger or irritation can be dissipated by the simple process of "sublimation", which means to "steam-off". This technique is positive thought action which if practised every time and with patience will quickly reduce all disturbing mental reactions. To apply this method you not only analyse but break down the anger by asking yourself the following questions. "If I must retaliate what emotional aspect of me will be pleased with itself – my pride, dignity, authority, social status or ego?" "When these emotional aspects have been satisfied will I have permanently solved the problem?" "If I retaliate in anger or violence where is the greatest damage inflicted – on myself or my opponent?" "Will anger or violence improve the situation or make it worse?"

"If my opponent insults me what aspect of me is really hurt – my pride, dignity or ego?" "If I respond with the higher (spiritual) mind my ego-self with its natural tendency for violence and revenge, which is more damaging to me, will be checked and subdued. Therefore, if I remain calm I will have achieved a spiritual victory over the lower-self". Your ego-mind may automatically supplant in your mind the worrying thought, "Your opponent will think you are cowardly, simple and stupid". This would not be true because it takes considerably more courage to decide on the spiritual course than the much easier egoistical, violent method in which the **cause** will remain. This reaction not only gives more power to the in-lying cause but further karmic causes are created which will inevitably have to be faced at some later date. The reader would be wise to retain the thought that compassion cures everything and condemnation creates nothing but further condemnation. Jesus put this truth in a much simpler way, "If your brother strikes you on one cheek offer him the other". His teaching was simple – to strike your brother automatically invites a return blow. This action, in turn, will provoke further blows so the pattern becomes increasingly worse. It will be impossible for this situation to improve or go away until love (the use of the spiritual mind) is offered in return for violence. Even if our opponent should pass out of our life, or environment, the damage and the karmic causes will still remain within both parties.

It might be thought, as you reflect on this teaching, how can anyone live a life of total pacifism; is it possible? In this hard, difficult world many people will take advantage of me and other people. The answer to these thoughts is simple. It is only impossible for the impermanent ego-self to live a life of pacifism.

As for the dangers of them taking advantage of you, only the ego-mind can be taken advantage of. As long as the thinker remains attached to the ego-mind it will use every means, search out every opportunity to persecute you. The rule of the arrogant ego-mind is, "When I am in command I am always right and you are always wrong. When Truth makes you stronger you will understand and tolerate me – for it is your duty to understand Truth. But whilst I am the stronger I shall continue to persecute you, for it is my duty to persecute ignorance".

The great mystical geniuses who reverenced human freedom and sought release from ego bondage, who taught the brotherhood of man, and the supremacy of Love and whose teachings have greatly enriched our earthly life taught us again and again, "The whole purpose of your existence in this impermanent world is to teach you, the Spirit, to die to the ego-man and to become detached from the object of this transient world. In nature's plan to free you from the impermanent world and self no experience is wasted or overlooked. For example your most difficult neighbour is also a most valuable teacher who is there because of the outworkings of the law of cause and effect. It is no accident but a planned situation in which nature sees an opportunity to help your progression. Nature sees only the spiritual side of man. Man is essentially and **eternally** pure spirit and nature's sole purpose is to reunite with the spiritual essence of man. Therefore, whenever man turns away from a spiritual course this is a direct transgression against the law of nature. This transgression will manifest in a variety of ways which will include disease, illness and other forms of suffering. It would serve the student well to remember, and believe, that no person has the power to create suffering within another person unless the latter **first** gives him the power. Whenever a person is experiencing suffering whether through a physical disturbance or through the actions of another person this is undoubtedly due to an imperfection (cause) lying within the soul.

This source of imperfection will always react to the actions of another person which could be for good or bad. All forms of suffering of the mind and physical are created **by the mind itself** and never by an outside cause. It should be apparent, from what has been said that the pattern of the mind holds the "seeds" which will flourish as good or bad actions and reaction. It is the law's purpose to use the soul "seed-patterns" of other persons to bring our bad areas to our attention. In this way **both** parties are given the same opportunities to recognise the disturbing causes within. No doubt one of the parties will simply discard the experience as an unfortunate accident or a brief disturbing encounter with a difficult person. This person may soon forget the incident as soon as their anger has died away, but the law will never forget because the same opportunity, or lesson, will return again and again until the inner cause is recognised. This recognition could take many days, months, years or another lifetime. By now the reader should have no good or valid reason for supposing that there are such things as accidents as regards illness and disease or other disruptive experiences. Every thought, action and reacton sets the law of cause and effect into action. Even though painful effects caused by direct physical means, such as accidents, the effects of consuming impure food and drink and casual injury are all the direct result of a disharmonious, careless mind. The

41

key to life's meaning and one which should be constantly before the mind of the reader is, "The mind in its right place will make a heaven out of hell, but when out of its rightful place can make a hell out of heaven".

The reader will now, I think, begin to realise that the incentive to **all** action is the search for happiness and security and the **only** difference between the progressing man and the materially attached man is that the former is searching the **natural** or correct way whilst the other is working in direct opposition to nature.

The reader should also have realised by now that the great root cause of all suffering and disease is, basically, **self-love,** and the only certain way to the relief of all suffering is, first, to understand the nature of self-love and its attachment to an impermanent world. Second, with this knowledge, together with an understanding of the needs of others, begin the process of detachment. The laws will continue to guide you, painful though some of the methods may be, towards the great ultimate – **the losing of our own interests.** Eventually we recognise that our own personal pains and suffering will never end until our feelings and thoughts flow **outwardly** towards humanity. Remember, disease, suffering and unpleasant experiences can only manifest on an **inward** flow to the self.

The Buddha taught that to live a life of attachment (self-love) is to condemn ourselves to three conditions: the constant change and impermanence of "things"; the illusion of the ego-self and, therefore, suffering. However, do not feel despair and hopelessness because of this statement. The vast majority of us have a very long way to go. Just as we cannot see the tiny seed growing we **know** it is growing. So the human seed – the soul – is growing even though we are not conscious of it. Happily, many students make remarkable progress, providing they keep in mind the teachings of the great masters of the world. In this way they will slowly add to their knowledge of the **nature of man** and the **nature of the world.** It is imperative – in fact it is inevitable – that they learn of both aspects of nature even though each pathway is directly opposed to the other. Only when this is accomplished will they begin to recognise their true spiritual identity and experience total freedom from suffering. In most of us there are many serious defects, or particularly strong attachments, which are hindering our development. It is these particular defects which we must seek out, recognise and overcome.

Naturally, many people will find this extremely difficult, or think impossible, but it is remarkably surprising how rapidly certain bad characteristics will diminish and finally disappear once they begin to use the simple exercises of "sublimation". The student should take heart from the fact that every attempt at sublimation **always results** in a degree of progress. If he perseveres failure is impossible. Once the student embarks upon this inner pathway of development he should always remember that **thought** is the supreme creative power which will not only speed his progress but will, in time, completely dissolve certain inner defects. For example, one of these defects could be a prevailing dislike for a particular person. In his case bring the thought to mind – that every human being, no matter how bad or evil is a divine creation. Within every soul there is the Divine Man, which is the **real** man. Through the constant action of this thought (cause and effect) not only will the defect slowly dissolve but the spiritual potential within the thinker will develop. Remember, every soul, no matter how base, is a potential saint. Try another simple thought exercise. Supposing you were walking along a street and without warning a person careers into you and perhaps knocks you to the ground. Your immediate reaction is one of anger until you notice that the person is totally blind. In an instant your anger disappears and is replaced by understanding because you have realised that you have encountered a **physical** cripple. Unfortunately, it is n ot so easy to recognise a **spiritual** cripple. Yet, all people who are living a life of self-love, reflecting greed, hate, jealousy, etc., are cripples of a more serious nature. Though the physical cripples need our understanding and physical assistance the spiritual cripples need our love and forgiveness much, much more because not only can love help him, but it is another opportunity provided by the law, to help yourself.

The quality of our thoughts constitutes our individuality. What makes some people good and others bad are the "ingredients", in other words, the motives, good and bad, and the desires within the soul. These are the forces behind the thought. Let us, therefore, take a closer look at the quality of some of these "ingredients" and decide what is good and how to replace the bad with good. Let us assume that pride is one of the ingredients. Now we must focus the power of meditative-thought on this defect. First consider where this sense of pride comes from. Consider now the nature of the source. It is impermanent, constantly changing in accordance with the nature of the object or incident which provoked the pride. The source cannot comprehend the nature of spirituality which is a state of **permanence.** Therefore, the source is empty of real power. Pride not only keeps the source in being but it damages its creator.

Take another example: a dislike of certain people or hate for a particular person. Think about love. Dislike and hate are the opposite of love. Think about Christ. Christ always saw good in every soul. "Judge ye not" he said "lest ye be judged". Love is the entire foundation of all creation. Love is the **only** way to dissolve the darkness of hate and dislike. As long as thoughts of dislike and hate remain within the mind all progress is at a standstill. Also bring to mind the thought that within you NOW resides your Higher Self. This inner, Higher Being – the real, undying you – realises nothing of pride, hate, cruelty, etc. These latter emotions are intruders within you – obsessive lodgers determined to oust the real owner which is you, the Higher Self. These "lodgers" will constantly direct your attention to justifiable motives and vengeful reactions and remind you of the similar ways of others for the purpose of convincing you of the correctness of your chastising ways.

It is not necessarily correct to be influenced by the wrongful ways of others. Unless, of course, they are "lost" and ask the way ahead. If a runaway vehicle is careering towards you it is your duty to stand aside and allow the vehicle to end up where it must. It would be foolhardy to stand in its way because it would be deaf to pleas. Many souls are like that runaway vehicle. They must be left alone for a while and allow the laws of experience to do their work first. As Jesus said, "There are sheep of another fold, but I will gather them in later". Before we start to replace hate and dislike with love we must first begin with our own individuality. Always remember that love creates love as hate does hate. The removal of other troublesome ingredients can only come about by directing **outwards** to others those thoughts of happiness, care and attention which we have been directing **inwards** to ourselves. If we have troubles, worries and anxieties it is not much use telling others about them because all we will get in return will be sympathy and impractical words of advice which will only alleviate our problems for a little while. At some later date they will return because the sympathy and the words did not remove the **cause** within us. The only positive way to remove these causes from the centre of our being is to direct outward, at every opportunity, consideration, tolerance and kindness to our fellow men in their hour of need. Spirit is love and the natural movement of love. In other words the spirit is an outward flow. Then all is harmony.

A disharmonious or unstable mind is always the cause of anxiety. To attempt to create with a disharmonious mind results in the disharmony being reflected into the work. The result, dissatisfaction all round. To correct a disharmonious mind requires a routine of mind discipline. No matter how simple or mundane the work is we have to approach it with a preconceived determination to do it as perfectly as possible. Spend some time considering how the work should be done then take one little step at a time. Be patient and keep the mind firmly focused upon the work and only the work. Thus you have created a state of harmony. Let us take an example of disharmony. We have decided to hang a picture on the wall. First we need a hammer and a nail. If we proceed to hammer the nail into the wall and we allow the mind to concern itself with another irrelevant problem we have created a state of disharmony. The inevitable result is that at some point we miss the nail and hit our finger. So the

45

effects of the disharmonious mind are reflected outwards and we end up with a very painful finger. The object of this little story is to emphasise that we cannot separate our mind from the action we are committed to. So in this way we can eradicate disharmony from the mind and likewise from our actions by focusing the mind on the task before us and consciously creating a sense of determination to do the work as neatly and cleanly as possible. Work slowly and take care that a sense of impatience is not allowed to creep in.

This vital mind exercise should not only be applied to material creations but also to our thoughts, words, expressions and manner. These characteristics also reflect our state of mind and can react on the other person. This is one of the most important lessons we have to understand. Jesus is depicted in the Bible as a carpenter. This is of symbolic importance. The Master – the perfect creator of all things, thoughts and motives. Master means complete mastery of the physical senses therefore the mind. The perfectly applied mind directs not only harmonious thoughts, words and expressions but also the instruments of the body. The spiritually controlled mind expresses itself equally in all things whether it be complex or childishly simple. In this mind there is no room for disharmony or instability – therefore, no room for suffering.

Every soul is born with some degree of ignorance. Nevertheless, ignorance is our vital teacher. It teaches us the errors of our ways and it prepares us for the necessary experiences which transform the ignorance into areas of wisdom. Therefore, do not be afraid of experience no matter how frightening. We should recognise that adverse and difficult circumstances are opportunities for great spiritual advances. Just as a particular kind of bee will be attracted to a particular flower so the right kind of experience will be directed to a particular area of ignorance. That is the supreme law, do not try to avoid it or fear it. This law will be fulfilled, it cannot be avoided indefinitely. It will help you to keep in mind that every aspect of experience unfailingly transforms an area of ignorance into wisdom. But, at the same time, **stay awake**, try to prevent the impulsive mind from making wrong decisions or retaliatory judgement. Always be prepared to expand the mind by applying the "sublimation" technique to every difficult, hurtful incident. Check the empty, distracting impulses of the ego-mind.

Each soul can only evolve according to the nature of the incoming experiences which are "tailor-made" for your particular progression. Apart from giving help and guidance whenever it is asked for and when it is needed each soul is responsible for their own progression. Concerning another soul we can do nothing more than to offer tolerance, kindness and love. It is not our duty to compel another person to do things acccording to our ideals or beliefs. He may have a totally different way to go so we should not distress ourselves or become unduly involved. With regard to the disturbances or difficulties which that person is experiencing his reactions to the difficulties may not only be your opportunity to express spirituality, but they may be the only way open to let in the love you are extending.

Greed is another form of self-love which means that our mind is completely controlled by the dictates of the five senses. The senses, sight, taste, hearing, touch and smell present the greatest obstacles to our advancement. Of course, the senses are divine gifts given to us to enjoy the things of nature. But ask yourself this vitally important question. Are you master of or slave to the senses? It is true that food and drink are essential for the sustenance and maintenance of the body, but do you eat and drink because it is healthy for the body or because you are addicted to the sensual experience it affords? All forms of addiction mean that the mind is firmly in the grip of desire therefore it is totally unconcerned as to whether the food and drink are good or bad for the body. Common examples are alcoholism and drug addiction. In these instances the mind is totally beyond the control of the spirit. Greed is a form of addiction which manifests in different ways. We can be greedy for food, drink, money, recognition, power, fame and attention. Each of these faults puts a stop to progress, creates fears, anxiety, insecurity and other harmful emotions. The damage, unforunately, is not entirely confined to ourselves. Our attitudes, emotions and actions do have a serious and sometimes a violent effect upon the development of those close to us and others whom we come into contact with. Never forget many of us have the power to create bad and violent emotions within others. We ourselves cannot possibly evolve until we are capable of helping other people by way of encouragement, providing hope, increasing knowledge etc. We must also show them tolerance, compassion and understanding.

When we are born into this world as innocent children we remain very close, spiritually, to the soul but as the awareness of the self develops we gradually become conditioned to the outside world on all levels, physical, emotional and intellectual. Very few people seriously ask themselves the question, "Why does this happen – why is the world like this and what is the purpose?" It begins because of our desire for inner happiness and security, but in reality it is the urgent call of the divine inner self for recognition. Unfortunately, at least for a time, we remain ignorant of the cause and so we plunge headlong into the world of opposites firmly believing we will find it. It will reward the student well to keep it in mind that all cravings and desires are the expressions of the self searching for this happiness but it learns again and again to its detriment that it cannot hold it permanently.

Greed is one of the densest of evils which conceals the way to permanent happiness, the Divine Self – our **true** nature. However, we must warn you again, though it is your duty, and an aid to your own progress, to give care, help, love and protection to a comrade you must never interfere with the natural progression of the other person. They have their own dictates of the soul, their own forthcoming experiences and to try to change this pattern would only invite frustration, anxiety and other disturbing thoughts to yourself. However, strive to develop growth in the other by **example** and give help when it is called for, but allow them full freedom. The law will never allow them to become totally lost. So in this way we are able to find out about our own faults which can be eliminated by creating the opposite emotion.

So in this way we patiently and conscientiously seek out the faults in our personality and "sublimate" them by the thought-analysis method already described. Only in this way are we able to eliminate causes of conflict between mind and soul replacing them with another inner-awareness to bring relief, harmony, health and happiness. The reader must most earnestly learn to develop this harmonious personality as only then will you be in accordance with the real nature of the soul.

You must be constantly alert to the selfish and thoughtless actions of others. These people can through their scorn, criticism, cruel and arrogant ways not only destroy your efforts but can place a tremendous strain upon your patience. Try to turn every difficult situation to your own advantage. In fact it would be extremely helpful to you in these situations to bring to mind three specific thoughts, one, they are presenting you with a testing specifically to meet the dictates of your soul and, two, remember no person has the power to hurt you unless you first give them the power, three, by remaining calm and deliberately curbing the mind's natural reaction to reply in what it may think is a justifiably reproachful manner. This attitude may later lead that person to a little gratitude or improved knowledge – just a little step, perhaps, on the road to spiritual understanding. To adopt such a philosophy means that we are slowly, but quite definitely, developing our individuality according to the directions of the soul.

Let no fear of any person enter our consciousness and make absolutely certain that no person is allowed to interfere with your development. Their interferences are not accidental, they are there for a purpose and the purpose is to help you. It may sound strange but their disruptive ways are actually a blessing in disguise because they are seeking out the faults in you. If you were entirely without faults you would not react in any way to their attitudes. Therefore, as long as you react, or **feel** like reacting, there is work to be done on your individuality. Remember the words of Krishnamurti, "We are today the product of our long past and we shall be tomorrow what we make of ourselves today".

I think we should also consider another helpful saying "Know to whom you have to speak". This means that we should be constantly on our guard as to whom we give advice and help. We must first be sure that the motive to help comes from our innermost self and not from the conceited ego-self in which case the words would fall on stony ground. Next we must make certain that the person is ready to receive our suggestions. If not, our approach could be resented or hurtful to the other person. Never forget every individual soul has its particular path to walk collecting experiences which are according to the dictates of that particular soul. We have no more right to divert that soul than someone else has to divert us. Never create fear or anxiety concerning someone else, no matter how they suffer. The laws never have them out of their sight and they will be allowed to go to the extreme limits of suffering, but they will never be allowed to go beyond that. Therefore, it is always a wise rule to advise and help only when it is asked for or when a person is seen to be incapable of helping themselves.

Also be aware of the person who is greedy for attention. This very often is seen with parents who for their own personal desires cling to their children. They selfishly instil into the children a false sense of duty whereby the offspring are prevented from fulfilling a particular ambition or perhaps from doing some great and useful work for the community. Many times parents, or other relatives, have unnecessarily used their invalidity, or feigned invalidity, when in fact the only fault was greed for attention. Many great ambitions have been denied, wonderful opportunities missed and much suffering created because a good, sensitive person has been completely dominated by one selfish person and they have not possessed the courage or willpower to demand their freedom.

Every soul has a duty to themselves and they are serving no good purpose whatsoever by allowing themselves to be dominated or allowing the selfish desires of the other to remain in being. We must courageously examine our own conscience and though we cannot ignore totally the plight of our patient, we must serve them in a way which helps them to overcome their problem. At the same time we must retain the freedom to follow the dictates of our own soul. Let us not fear to plunge into this problem. We are here to gain experience from every situation and every person and it serves no purpose whatsoever to ignore any problem. It is our duty to gather the truths of nature and humanity, and our relative who is greedy for attention could be a fine teacher.

Those who are greedy for attention are as little children. Therefore, our attitude should be as if we were administering to a child. Remember that to lose control of our individuality, that is allowing constant interference with the development of our own personality and freedom of action, can prove to be extremely debilitating, bring about anxiety complexes followed by exhaustion and possibly illness. Like a very young child they have a simple form of consciousness. In which case, for our patient as well as for the child, our approach to the problem should be to give all the spiritual, mental and physical guidance to the utmost of our ability. Always remembering that both the patient and the child are individual souls who are on earth to gather experience and knowledge. So, whilst we must retain our own freedom we must do all in our power to teach the others independence and to help them to establish their own individuality.

At no time will this venture prove to be easy or straight-forward. Many times the patient, like the child, will demand your attention and angrily denounce you, very often, as being selfish and cruel because you are not giving in to all their demands. Never allow this interference to distract you from your purpose but always remain calm, patient and only helpful when the situation complies with the dictates of the treatment. For that is exactly what it is – **treatment.** But you must be careful about your attitude towards the treatment and be sure that you do not apply them simply because they are more convenient to yourself – this could be a subtle form of selfishness. Watch carefully for any sign of dominance on **your** part and, if necessary, check it immediately. This attitude of greed can be extremely subtle and can, unwittingly, manifest in unspiritual forms, such as attempting to change the will, ideals or desire of another, manipulating the circumstances to gain for yourself added comfort. It could be a form of escapism from boredom, or difficult or embarrassing situations, etc. Always strive to encourage within yourself the spiritual art of giving, patience, tolerance and understanding. We must continue to develop these attributes until by frequent acts of self-sacrifice we eliminate every cause which is likely to create harmful, adverse actions.

Many homes which have children, or persons hungry for attention, have become some kind of prison because those living there have created attitudes and behavioural reactions calculated to maintain a false kind of peace, or avoid some form of unpleasantness. These enforced and unnatural attitudes make personal freedom impossible, severely cramps individual life-styles, prevents normal development of the personality and generally brings unhappiness to everyone involved. It is not surprising therefore, that from these difficult conditions mental, emotional and physical disorders arise.

Of course, it is true that it may be the calling of one individual to devote his or her life entirely to another in which case there is happiness and love. But it must be made certain that his kind of relationship has not developed because one person was exceptionally weak, the other very dominant and persuaded the first, against their better judgement, that it was their Christian duty to take care of them. The real truth is that it is the committed duty of every soul to come to earth to fight battles, to understand and finally overcome the giants of illusion and the attachments of the lower ego-self which are the cause of all illnesses, diseases and suffering. On this battlefield we will meet many people whose object is to possess, dominate, deter us and to convince us that we are on the wrong track. Each one must be faced, experienced, tested and overcome. We are ever the warrior but we do not fight. We use only the weapon of "sublimation". The greatest battlefield and one where the biggest battles are fought is very often in our own homes, but always remember victories of self-freedom are **never** won in anger, by personal judgement and condemnation, by impatience or running away. Involve yourself in the battle but do not fight. Only the technique of sublimation will free you permanently from adverse domination and the "imprisonment" of the home, community, office or society.

It cannot be stressed too much that every soul must look upon their opponent, or oppressor, not as an enemy, but as an opportunity to overcome some of our weaknesses. These so-called difficult people are like a light in the darkness they illuminate our faults. As long as our faults or weaknesses remain hidden to us we can never evolve.

Therefore, if it were not for our "opponents" we would be denied the opportunities to develop courage, individuality and knowledge to free ourselves from all suffering. The real victories come from the wisdom of the spirit (the real, permanent self) through love, tolerance, forgiveness, kindness, patience and gentleness. Force simply creates force, violence creates further violence. These are very hard lessons to understand, let alone apply but the ignorance is only as deep as the attachment of the ego-self is strong. Our only duty, no matter who we are, king or beggarman, is to overcome the dominance of the ego-self because as long as it reigns we shall only know disease and suffering.

Those who are dominant and selfish require your help. They are the **spiritual** cripples. Another dominant, selfish person cannot help them, they can only make the situation worse. Therefore the **only** ones who can help are those who, like yourself, allow the spirit within to speak and act. The spirit has only one voice, yet it is the most powerful voice in existence, the voice of love and understanding. If any reader should disbelieve this then they are lending their ear to the ego-mind. The ego-mind knows nothing of love, understanding, compassion or sacrifice – it thinks only about itself. Whoever walks this pathway needs lots of courage and faith, but remember, no soul is ever given more than it can accomplish. The spirit within you is all-powerfull, it **never** leaves you and no matter how deep the darkness it remains closer to you than your heart-beat. At this point I invite the reader to spend the next few moments in quiet contemplation. First, realise that we are body, soul and spirit. The body is temporal therefore whatever it accomplishes must be temporal.

Much like a bar of chocolate (symbolic of all sense objects), the body desires it, the body consumes it after which there is nothing left, just a memory. Soul and spirit are eternal, they are love and unity. Therefore, whatever they accomplish is eternal, because they accomplish only in love and understanding. Imagine that a very angry person is approaching you because you have something of a material nature belonging to him, or perhaps you have unconsciously said something which was misunderstood or hurtful. We have only two courses of action open to us. We can reply in the same angry voice, in which we are defending the impermanent ego, in which case physical violence could follow. So the situation is made more ugly and impossible. Or, we can remain calm, smile, apologise and offer the hand in friendship. In nearly every case the angry man will quieten down, the fire will be removed from the mind and the situation will generally become much calmer. This will be a victory for your inner-self and a defeat for the ego-mind. Such a lesson Jesus taught, "If your brother strikes you on one cheek, offer him the other". We cannot stress enough how difficult these lessons are to accept and apply, but when you think about it, there is no other **permanent** solution. But, then, the permanent solution is always the most difficult. The impermanent way is always the easiest but the most cowardly.

Jesus said, "Judge ye not lest ye be judged". In other words are we so perfect that we can afford to condemn others? Therefore, we should never speak against men who, according to our inner-wisdom, are living the wrong kind of life. Many of these people are totally unaware, as yet, of the right way of life. The little seed deep in the ground cannot be condemned for denying that there is a heavenly sun existing above its darkness. We must patiently wait because, first, the seed needs the conditions of darkness, the loneliness and other adverse conditions to help its progress. Only after these experiences will it realise that there is a heavenly light. The human soul is also a seed. The man who is searching for relief from the adversities of a physical life will find many wrong turnings and, understandably, react wrongly, sometimes violently, against the constant frustrations. They are blind like the seed and have no understanding of the reason and purpose of life. He is not our enemy but a lost friend who is desperately seeking a better way of life. In time he will learn that he is searching in the wrong direction. But, at least, give him the opportunity (as you were given) to examine every possible way right **and** wrong. Many of my readers have, hopefully, begun to recognise the right way, therefore **you** are not only his only hope but the hope for the whole of humanity.

The immutable laws which unerringly guide us through every situation are truly amazing. Not a single incident or iota of energy is neglected or wasted. The man who is groping blindly in the darkness of ignorance is not only giving us the opportunity to serve the spirit but his experiences are used to help us to climb higher and higher. The help you are giving him now will enable him to help others in the same way sometime in the future. Never forget, where you are today is the result of the help someone else, higher up the scale, gave you sometime in the past. Humanity is like a huge chain we are all dependent upon those above and those below.

Disease, illness and suffering are our common enemies and the only way we can prevent the spread of these maladies is **first** to clear them out of ourselves by not becoming involved in those conflicts between mind and soul which provide all the necessary power to keep disruption in being.

If our own soul is diseased how can we spread health? This achievement will be a supreme victory and we will be in a powerful position to he!p others not by handing out instructions or preaching **but by our examples**. That is the entire secret of healthy souls and of spreading health. There will be no need for drugs, chemicals or medicines – the temporal reliefs! It is not really as difficult as it first appears. As long as each soul makes a little effort every day, watches for every opportunity to serve each day, the effect upon the whole of humanity could be enormous – but, more important, upon you.

I have one or two friends who are classified as "millionaires". They have beautiful homes, many luxuries, motor cars, servants and enjoy the best of foods. They are not to be despised for their wealth or their luxurious way of life. They can be princes, they can be godsends because they employ many hundreds of people. They provide these people with money, food, homes and the vital necessities of life. Supposing these millionaires had chosen to join a monastery? There would have been just that little bit more misery and poverty added to life. Life, as Jacob's dream suggested to us, is a vast ladder – a mystical ladder – ascending from earth to heaven. On every rung of that ladder from the lowest to the highest a number of souls were standing. Every level of consciousness (already within the human soul) must be filled and known by every soul. Each level has something to teach us and each level places us in situations which will be of the very best advantage to us. The divine laws which guide us never make a mistake, but know exactly from which position we can best serve ourselves and our brothers. There are saints in the market place and the high street as well as in heaven. Knowing this there should be no place for envy, greed or jealousy in our personality. It is as the Commandments tell us, "Thou shalt not covet thy neighbour's house, his wife or his manservant nor anything that is thy neighbour's".

There is a general feeling afoot that disease, especially cancer, is on the increase. Certainly psychiatrists and neurophysicians tell us that mental disease is greater now than it has ever been. When we stop to consider this and think about possible explanations there is one positive explanation which not only offers an answer but confirms quite definitely the principal message conveyed in this book. For almost two thousand years Western civilisation has become more and more sophisticated. What is thought to be more and better ways of living have been developed. Science has speeded up our life generally with the result that more and more "labour-saving" machines have become a "natural" part of our life. We have saved time only to find that there are many more things to do and still not enough time to do them. In truth, we have entered into an intense period of materialism. The mind of man has been totally occupied with means and ways of getting more and more possessions, achieving greater ambitions, seeking out ways of experiencing more sensual pleasures. In other words, the transient things have taken over from the real things of life. The real purpose of man's incarnation has been taken over by an endless chain of desire to gather more and more of the world's glittering treasures around him. The real strengths, the permanent comforts and the unfailing spiritual upliftments which come from the awareness of our true unchangeable nature have been blocked and replaced by anxiety for the future, the uncertainty of achieving our ambitions and the fears that inevitably arise from all things which are temporal.

The true nature of our inner self, the positive direction indicated clearly by the soul's dictates, also the guide and unerring stimulus of our every action has been repressed and replaced by superficial things and the ego-self's feverish efforts to find comfort in earthly pleasures and illusive compensations for our failings and trials. So thus has the human race entered into a frenzied race for wealth, position, fame and worldly possessions. As all of these things are impermanent, illusory and can only be obtained and held by anxiety, effort, fear and continuous, concentrated desire, so there is no place in the soul for internal peace.

Happily, the age of materialism is beginning to reach its peak. People are beginning to question the **literal** meanings of religion and wish to look deeper. There is undoubtedly a slight awakening within and a desire for "something" more real, more reliable. In countries all over the world seminars are catering for a rapidly growing number of people who are desiring knowledge about life after death, reincarnation, ways of defeating disease by spiritual methods, searching out the ancient teachings and wisdom of the East. The pendulum of the world is now slowly swinging back and away from pure materialism – the soul of the world is now rising! The world is rapidly reaching the point when the problem of disease and illness, including mental illness, will have to be looked at in a totally different way from that of gross materialism. Doctors, scientists and psychiatrists must become aware of the divine laws which govern and control every aspect of nature including our inner as well as the outer world.

The art of healing must, sooner or later, pass out of the monopolising hands of doctors, surgeons and psychiatrists to the divine domain of spiritual, soul and mental healing. When the physicians fully realise that the entire cause of illness and disease lies in the materially aroused conflict between mind and soul and that they must lay aside their drugs and medicines and concentrate upon restoring the harmony between these two aspects only then will they understand the deeper meaning of Plato's immortal words, "Never attempt to heal the body until you first heal the mind".

Of course it would be foolhardy to assume that the time will eventually come when there will be no need for doctors, surgeons or psychiatrists. There will always be people who will remain attached to the mentally and physically disturbing things of the earth. There will always be the sudden accidents which will need the services of the surgeon, but the principal theme of this book is to familiarise the medical profession with the **spiritual** advances and growth of certain people and to bring to their attention the reality of the inner **causes** which **must** be observed first to bring about a permanent cure of the body. Already the gift of spiritual healing is passing into the hands of various religious healers and into those of the specially gifted healer who is practising unobtrusively and virtually ignored by the majority of doctors. So it seems that the doctors and the psychiatrists of the future will have to develop two different approaches to illness. First the doctor and psychiatrist will necessarily have to be dedicated students of the basic philosophy and purpose of life so that he can enlighten his patients with knowledge of the law of cause and effect; point out to him the fundamental **causes** lying within the soul which are creating the disruptive conflicts between mind and soul.

The patient will be instructed to remedy these causes himself. Secondly, the physician should be able to advise his patient how to bring about the necessary harmony. In other words the patient must be prepared to adopt an entirely different way of thinking and, therefore, living. The patient must also be encouraged to develop and perform certain virtues to clear away the causes. Naturally each and every patient will need a careful study of every aspect of his life and I am absolutely certain that this will demand the training of a special class of doctor who will necessarily devote his life to a study of spiritual philosophy and the evolution of mankind. He will need to be an advanced teacher of the purpose of our existence and the reason for the need for experience. Of course, there will always be a time when the physical body will need attention therefore the doctor will need to be versed in certain natural remedies which would include balanced diets and specific herbs. This was strongly advocated by Hippocrates who stated, "For every disease there is a natural remedy".

So, it appears that the conquest of illness is entirely left in the hands of the individual being given moral support and encouragement, of course, by an enlightened doctor or healer. The individual must be fully conversant with the immutable laws which govern his body and the entire universe. But more important he must be totally obedient to these laws, live strictly in accordance with the rules, to realise that the slightest transgression will mean pain and suffering, otherwise, he can achieve a life of great joy, peace and happiness. The advent of the special physician will open an entirely different field of rehabilitation. His work will be to impart truth and purpose to the patient's existence, give the necessary support and encouragement and instill into him a belief in the great divine power.

I think, by now, we have proved the point that illness and all forms of suffering begin because of a persistent conflict between mind and soul. Therefore on this premise if we work to achieve a personality which remains free of conflict it is possible to

59

establish an inner immunity from illness and disease. Just as we envelop our bodies with clothing to keep out cold and atmospheric debris so we must learn to clothe our mind with a "protective" awareness to keep out conflicts arising between the ego-mind and the things of the world. Mind is an extremely complex instrument but basically it is divided into the "Higher-Reaches" and the "lower-levels". The "lower-levels" are closely linked with the physical senses which are constantly in communication with the outer-world. Mind on the higher reaches is the "illuminated" mind which views the great **indefinable** experiences such as love, inspiration, intuition and compassion, but its function is also to provide **understanding** of the lower mind. Life as we experience it must be regarded as an inseparable organic association of mind with matter. If it were possible to separate mind from matter, matter would automatically lose all the characteristics of life. In other words, we would simply be left with a complex collection of chemicals and minerals. This is exactly what happens when the body "dies". The higher mind can "understand" the lower and can, at times, inspire the lower order because it is a fact that we do fluctuate between the two minds. No person is completely ignorant of the spirit, nor totally evil, but the ability of the lower mind attempting to understand the higher is an impossible one.

The fluctuation between the higher and the lower mind differs from person to person according to their scale of enlightenment. The more evolved a soul is the more the thought is inclined to pass **from the higher** to the lower whereas with a less evolved soul the thought will pass not too frequently **from the lower** to the higher.

When we consider the real permanent values in human life – the joy of appreciating beauty, the inner love for all things of nature including for each other, compassion, the illuminating joy of inspirational thought – the ability of the lower mind to express them is virtually impossible. The lower mind cannot understand the nature or origin of goodness, unselfishness or self-sacrifice. Only the higher reaches of the mind understands these indefinables because they are the **source**. These expressions of the higher order – love, truth, spiritual beauty, etc., are the emanations of the pure mind the result of the perfect harmony between mind and soul. At this spiritual level there is absolute unity with the **real** values of life but at the lower mental levels there is a closer association with the physical levels. Truths of the spirit cannot filter through mind conditioned by ideals, thoughts and desires. Each soul, therefore, according to its degree of evolution can only reach to the height where it is capable of recognising truth. If the soul is well developed it will discover the power within to recognise the difference between the promptings of the ego-mind and the wisdom of the higher mind. The sole purpose of our existence, then, is to strive to lift the function of the mind beyond the disturbing and troublesome levels so that it eventually understands and **controls** the lower, and is able to express truth of a higher order. Browning the great philosopher and poet recognised this truth and so wrote:-

"Truth is within ourselves: it takes no rise
From outward things whatever you may believe
There is an innermost centre within us all
Where truth abides in fullness; and around
Wall upon wall, the gross flesh hems it in
This perfect, clear perception – which is Truth".

The reader should set aside a short period each day to be totally alone in as quiet a place as possible; be sure there will be no interruptions, then quietly think about yourself. Bring to mind all the disruptive actions you had performed that day. Then think about your persistent faults including all the bad habits you had accumulated in your life. Contemplate the source of these actions. The reasons why they developed. Was it your pride, ego, possessiveness or dignity? What would have been the end result of your action? Would it have made you a better person spiritually? What part of you wanted satisfaction? Would there have been a **permanent** solution to the **cause** of the action? Was it a kind thing you did or hurtful? Did you leave the other person as a friend or an enemy? If you left as enemies bring to mind the truth that the **cause** of the problem is not only

61

still there but has developed.

This self-analysis is an honest attempt to recognise the nature of the lower or ego-self which is the first step towards the higher levels of mind. Be patient, do not expect to make rapid progress or see results within a few days. But every time self-analysis is practised some definite progress is made. Never attempt to suppress anything. Suppression is similar to locking the thought away in a cupboard in the mind, but you have to remember to keep the door locked. Bring everything clearly out in the open thus we eventually wash from our personality slowly but surely all traces of mind-soul conflict.

CHAPTER THREE

ILLNESS LIES IN THE
NATURE OF OUR FAULTS

Whenever a real fault in our personality is sensed the way to eliminate this is to decide not to give battle to the fault, this simply creates further conflict. Forget about whether you have sufficient willpower and just quietly sublimate by analysing the fault, after which contemplate the opposite or spiritual virtue. Then analyse the opposite virtue; its origin and nature. This is the only natural and permanent method of removing faults and reducing conflicts. Another approach to reducing faults is to study the illness or physical disruption. Then bring to mind as many emotional conditions and conflicts as possible and try to work out which of these disturbances could have been responsible for your illness or mental disturbance.

Perhaps one of the biggest conflicts you have and the one which is most likely the cause of headaches, indigestion and loss of energy is boredom. Boredom is probably one of the greatest tragedies for those who rely totally upon the things of the material world for their enjoyment. Entertainment, though very useful at times to bring temporal relaxation, should not be allowed to become a regular habit because it is an **inward** experience and therefore a transient action. Once we begin to rely upon someone else, or something, to help us to escape from certain of our trials we become attached, or addicted, to an exhausting circle of getting nowhere. Relaxation and amusements are always good for us but not when they are used to shut out problems and worries from our mind. You can always maintain a balance by taking part in some activity which is helpful or brings happiness and relief to another. When entertainments are used for escapism not only must they be repeated but the form must be changed often because yesterday's joys soon become today's bore. So we continue to seek forms of play until they in turn become boring. Joys received from the **outside** are always shortlived. These forms of pleasure are usually sought for in nightclubs, bars, parties and in sensual pleasures experienced during certain depraved practices.

Therefore, the answer to boredom, which is a malady of the ego-self, is to take an interest in all things which promote the **outward** flow from the higher mind to all possible activities going on around us. For instance, youth clubs, age concern groups, local community activities, seminars, health clubs and sport organisations. Learn as much as you can about your fellow man and from nature. Watch for opportunities when you can use your knowledge and skills to the advantage of a fellow traveller. As you develop these faculties you will discover that you are slowly achieving a sense of satisfaction and joy from everyday occurrences which previously were missed, or simply dismissed, as a waste of time. The simple things in life, a kind word, a smile, a helping hand add up to the real satisfying pleasures of life because the simple things are very close to the soul – the Great Truth.

Fear is one the the greatest sorrows of human life. Fear is unnatural. It is born of a deep sense of insecurity. The lower self is afraid of losing its temporal possessions, physical companionship, its power, authority and recognition. It is totally ignorant of the fact that man is destined to lose **everything** that is of a transient nature.

The nature of man is eternal and essentially a spiritual being. The spirit is on a positive return journey – back to the reality of the deep unchanging inner self. As only the absolute pure spirit can blend with the pure spirit the laws of experience are watchful that we leave behind, bit by bit, every earthly attachment including ambition. The Great Laws help us in every way to do this. The Bible tells us, "It is easier for a camel to walk through the eye of a needle than for a rich man to enter into the Kingdom of Heaven". The rich man is he who has many attachments, desires and ambitions. The law never ceases to operate through our life and most people remain totally ignorant of this. The Laws compel us to make sacrifices which appear to be cruel, heartless and without purpose. But these experiences are made because very often we do not have the courage nor the wisdom to make the necessary changes ourselves. Fear is one of the most fundamental causes of illness because it is a prevailing, debilitating, emotional stress. When we experience fear it is the lower-mind which creates then nurtures the emotion until it is eventually erupting through the physical. The lower mind is only capable of being aware of the transient world and instinctively it knows that the objects of this world upon which its existence depends have but a limited life span. The insatiable desire of the lower self to preserve the **status quo** on all physical and mental levels calls for the maintenance of a continuous supply of objects. In many instances the pressure and the responsibility to meet this demand creates the utmost anxiety. In reality, no aspect of fear holds any place in the true, or immortal, nature of man. The essential man is permanent but the world around him is temporal. Therefore, the world of "things" has no power at all to overcome the permanent nature of man.

Working side by side with the supreme Laws which constantly and unfailingly watch over the advancement and guidance of the immortal man are also the lesser natural laws which govern the rise and fall of the objective world. The spiritual laws because of their permanent nature could not allow the lesser laws to over-burden and eventually eliminate the existence of the essential being. Nevertheless we are living in an age of expanding materialism and fear naturally increases as our increasing desires add to our possessions be they external riches or the fulfilment of ambitions. As the transient nature of these things make them so difficult to obtain and once obtained can only be held, or experienced, for very short periods this naturally arouses further anxieties. For example, the fear of losing our possessions and the added fear of not being capable of obtaining further supplies. Never at any time in the world's history has there been such a tremendous demand upon the services of psychiatrists, psychotherapists and psychologists because this is the age of fear which has developed to such a degree that it has become one of the major powers for harm. As **all** fears are created by self-interest no other motives have greater power for creating and intensifying disease and illness.

One established fact, proven in the field of psychiatry, is that people who are earnestly and enthusiastically absorbed in work concerning the welfare of others have a much lower rate of illness than those who spend their time creating anxieties concerning their own welfare. The former literally have no time to send thoughts inward regarding their own **possible** illness or failures. There is another fact which has escaped the attention of most people and that concerns bacteria and various germs associated with infectious diseases. It is noticed that those enthusiastically involved in creative projects designed to give pleasure and enjoyment, and this includes those engaged in welfare work, are seldom infected even though they are exposed to the same possibilities as others. Scientists have, so far, failed to give a satisfactory explanation for this extraordinary phenomenon. But then many men engaged in quantitative science have no knowledge of the powers of the Higher-Self which in the ordinary course of man's life is capable of protecting and affording adequate immunity to those who are consciously working in unison with it. The love of creativity, of providing and caring for others, is not only the positive application of these spiritual forces, but it is also a natural outflowing of the inner-beings. Fear and anxiety, on the other hand, being an inward flow and being an unnatural action have a depressing effect on our mental, therefore general nervous system.

Every creation of nature, throughout the animal, vegetable and mineral world, when not depressed or misused by the objective world, is in a perfect state of harmony. Germs and bacteria and **natural** forms of living organisms by themselves cannot create epidemics. All physical bodies have a built-in defence system, directed and powered by the higher-self. Therefore as the real cause of illness and disease is the conflict we introduce into our own personality, which suppressed the forces of the higher self, then no one has reason to go about fearing an infection because the prevention already lies within ourselves. If we put aside all fear of physical contact being the sole cause of making us ill and, at the same time, remain aware that it is fear, anxiety or the **anticipation** of disease which renders us susceptible we can walk safely through the greatest epidemic.

No one should ever become too anxious about their body. It is simply a vehicle which conveys the soul from educational experience to educational experience. But like all vehicles they need a certain amount of care and maintenance. Internal and external cleanliness is naturally important. Flesh is a special fabric which, like all fabrics, needs attention according to its nature. All vehicles need fuel so there is a special fuel for each type of vehicle. The body being a natural creation needs natural food and fuel. No one would dream of putting water into a gasolene driven motor, but water is the only natural fluid for the physical body. Everyone notices the car which is loved by its owner. It always looks clean, shiny and beautiful and it continues to operate efficiently much longer than the neglected model of the same year. The physical body is many times stronger and much more complex than the modern motor car. Nevertheless, it is persistently mis-used, given the wrong food and drink. It is not surprising there comes the time when it suffers a breakdown. The natural foods for the body are clean and wholesome such as fresh fruit, vegetables and clean water drunk as frequently as possible.

Other drinks such as tea, coffee and alcohol are not natural drinks but the body will tolerate them when not in excess. Animal flesh is not natural food for human and certain animal bodies. An examination of the intestines of vegetable eating animals (including the human being) and the carnivorous animals reveal significant differences. The carnivores have a comparatively short intestine. Consumed flesh putrifies very rapidly in warm, moist interiors and must, therefore, be evacuated fairly quickly from the animal's body. Whereas vegetables need a much longer time to be broken down in the stomach until the nutrients can be extracted. So the vegetable eating animals have an extraordinarily long intestine. Moderate exercise, such as walking, swimming and yoga are of course extremely beneficial to the blood circulation.

By now the reader should have realised that the truths concerning our health have been reiterated in many ways throughout this book. But principally our freedom from illness and disease depends solely upon the following. First, to realise that every being is body, soul and mind (or spirit). Soul and mind, in the higher reaches, is the higher self – the vital life-force. It is the source of love, compassion, creativity and is the origin of the **outward** flowing spiritual power. This source has total power to overcome all physical and mental conflicts providing the power is encouraged to flow according to its natural pathway. All gentle, loving, spiritual expressions extended towards another are outward and devoid of conflict. Second, to realise that the body itself is totally incapable of creating disease or infection; that all diseases are the result of an unnatural **inward** flow which is the conflict between mind and soul. All conflicts are expressions of anti-spiritual actions and reactions including physical, vocal, behaviour and thoughts. Third, our willingness and ability to recognise faults within our own personality which are creating the conflicts. And, finally, the determination to patiently use the "sublimation" technique to eliminate the faults and to respond with spiritual reactions when experiencing the unspiritual approaches of another.

The human body has innumerable organs the functioning of which are totally independent of man's normal consciousness. This enables the body to continue its vital maintenance and functions even when sudden physical and environmental changes take place. For example, when the body is rendered unconscious the important life-supporting organs continue to work. These hidden resources are so powerful that it is unusual for them to be unequal to any task or for a total breakdown to supervene. Even behind these resources there are other powerful reserves which automatically come into action. Therefore, given a reasonable chance the body can readapt and recover from most disturbances.

Our emotional and mental life is continuously conditioning our physical body **below** the normal level of consciousness (subconsciousness) with the result we come to accept, unfortunately as normal, conflicting conditions as a necessary struggle for any degree of achievement. The Hebrew poet and philosopher, who said, "Every valley shall be exalted and every mountain and hill made low" was actually describing the conscious reaction, on all levels, to life's dramas – the adoption of calmness, peace, harmony and tranquillity. Thus, come what may, leave the wiser, inner nature alone and the easiest, most enjoyable levels across the valleys and mountains of life will always be found. However uncomfortably challenging the way ahead may appear to be, calmly accept it as another opportunity and the one way offered to us to progress.

Try to realise that you are in a friendly universe and that you are embarking upon a necessary, vital and intelligent pilgrimage and that at the very heart of yourself there is the indestructible soul – the powerful, unwavering, ever-loving guide. No great journey of discovery was ever made without faults. They must be accepted as very important experiences which will help us never to fall into the same pits again. Never allow the mind to dwell upon mistakes made in the past. Have no regrets or remorse. The mistakes no longer exist because the ignorance which created them has been transformed into wisdom. Never look back because like Lot's wife you will become rooted to the ground like a pillar of salt. All fears of the future must be cast out of the mind because the future does not exist. The inner intelligence has already made plans of which you are not yet aware.

If you already have an illness, it may appear to you to be cruel, unjustified and unnecessary, but remember the words of Krishna, "For whenever righteousness decays and there is a rising up of evil, these myself I do create". In other words, disease is the penalty of wrong thought and wrong action. The cause of **all** our troubles is self-centredness and separation from

69

the outward flow of our own spiritual powers. Our health, happiness and harmony depend always and only on the nearness of our personality to soul and mind. The closer the union the greater the peace within us and to those around us.

Transformation of inner-energy for outer-health

To develop the greatest potentialities of the physical and mental bodies we must develop the technique of effecting the transformation of vital energy from the highest reaches of the mind particularly for the operation of potent healing forces. This is not only for the benefit of our own health but also to bring health to others. According to the great Masters of yoga techniques the achievement and preservation of the body in health as a harmonious vehicle is gained through psycho-physical techniques involving various forms of mental concentration. Their aim is to arouse energising powers lying latent in the higher mind. When through patience and practice they are effectively aroused certain organs are energised also other centres which are disturbing the body.

The essential disciplines designed to bring the mind completely under the control of the Will so that we achieve a highly efficient instrument of spiritual consciousness are:- (1) Total concentration (2) Meditation and (3) Contemplation. For all these practices the correctness of posture is essential. Though the classic cross-legged posture (Lotus) has its advantages it is not essential. Sitting on the floor or on a chair with crossed ankles, wrists resting on knees is quite effective providing the spine is kept erect. It will be of little benefit to attempt meditation lying in bed or seated in an easy chair as this suggests the idea of comfort and sleep. There are many meditational techniques but it is only necessary to concentrate upon one. Each technique is simply another exercise in concentration to bring the restless mind under the control of the Will. Only then are we able to enter into meditation.

It is the nature of the surface mind, or ego, to jump from one concept, or thought, to another and it is very difficult to place the undisciplined mind where one wants it to be and to keep it there. For too long our mind has been without control. It is impulsive in action, quick to judge and condemn. Therefore, it has become an inefficient instrument. We have, in the past, attempted very little real (spiritual) thinking with the result that most of our thinking has been highly coloured by ego-emotions. Always begin contemplative meditation with a few moments of rhythmic breathing. This will help most people to reach a state of mental quietness. Now begin the practice of concentration. Place an image before the mind's eye. This may be anything; a flower, crucifix, a star, the outline of Christ, any holy figure or anything of a spiritual nature. Whatever the image make it simple but try to create it in colour and with some detail. Be warned, the first attempts to keep the image in mind always end in failure. Without, at first, realising it the image will have been pushed out of mind and taken over by an everyday type of thought. These interruptions will continue for several weeks, even months. Never, never get impatient, frustrated or allow a sense of determination to enter the mind. Do not allow the mind to dwell upon the problems of the interruptions. Continue to bring back the image to the mind's eye. Once a student went to Sri Ramakrishna complaining he could not control the intruding thoughts. Ramakrishna replied, "Bringing the mind back **again** and **again** to the image that **is** meditation". The Bhagavad Gita also recommends that it does not matter very much if the mind wanders off in the beginning, so long as you bring it back. If we can remember that then half the battle is won.

Unfortunately, we do not always follow this advice but keep the mind on the problem of the interruptions and so believe we have failed and the quest is given up. Always remember, whenever you bring the mind back to the image that **is** success. We have taken another small step forward. Try to keep the mind relaxed and unrestrained.

For many weeks or months it will appear that the results are negligible, but this will be a mistake – an illusion. Experienced teachers tell us that perseverance **is always** rewarding. In time, you will discover the mind has less and less tendency to wander off. Always be aware of the temptations of the ego-mind. It distrusts spiritual ventures and will do everything in its power to put you off the track. Many times it will refuse to settle down and remains restless with all kinds of thoughts. Some of these thoughts will suggest, "It is no use you meditating; your mind is not sufficiently spiritual: You have a low state of mind it will take years. You are not the right kind of person' and so the thoughts will go on. When these thoughts interrupt you and you begin to have doubts just bring to mind the fact that every spiritual teacher and Master had to experience the same disruptive thoughts and tricks.

The practice of concentration, when it is beginning to be successful, diminishes the sense of effort and the feeling of failure until the mind is in unity with the thought-image. This is just the beginning of the deeper stage of meditation. When you reach this point the mind is not active but unusually calm and still. After further practice a higher level of spiritual mind gradually illuminates the lower levels with profound insights, intuitive knowledge and "wordless" wisdom. This is followed by an enhanced sense of freedom, inner power and wholeness. Having reached this degree of development the student requires no further instruction from any outside source because the greatest teacher of all – his inner intuition – takes complete charge of him. The intuition faculty is the wisdom of the spiritual consciousness and contains all that has ever been learned and collected as wisdom through all existences of the mind-soul and the ego-mind.

Periodically the student should subject himself to the discipline of **self-observation.** This technique is based upon the fact that far too long we have been immersed in the ways and demands of the ego-mind and we have repeatedly failed the earnest promptings of the spiritual self. With the result we have remained blind to the existence of a higher and more powerful self. Sit quietly as if in meditation and dwell with some concentration on the idea that the self-control and self-development of your inner spiritual qualities have a far greater significance than the attainment of worldly goods or ambitions.

Then consider the limited life-span of the goods and ambitions compared with the infinite life and power of the inner-self. Power which **already** lies within you. Consider which aspect of the lesser-self you are prepared to renounce immediately. You should commence with the simpler habits.

You must always guard against the sudden emotional actions of the impulsive mind. These responses have developed into an automatic reaction, or habit, when confronted by an awkward situation or person. During such a confrontation watch for the responsive emotion within and should it be one of anger, hate, jealousy etc., then contemplate it for a while. Decide which mind will be allowed to act – the spiritual or the ego-mind. Decide positively it must be the spiritual and refuse to allow anger to be the judge. At first, it may not be easy to keep control, but the important thing is to keep making the attempt every time. Every attempt is a positive step in the right direction. Sometimes you will succeed and other times you will fail, but eventually (and this is certain) you will achieve the ability to identify and control all impulsive emotions.

After further attempts another development will take place. You will **intuitively** recognise that the spiritual-mind and the ego-mind are two distinctly separate things and you have the ability to separate them. The wrong kind of emotions will quickly be overcome by "mentally" asking information concerning their source, objective and their actual worth in the long run. No emotions are more damaging to the soul (therefore the body) than hatred, jealousy, cruelty and anger. Thus, by separating the two minds and examining the emotions objectively and analysing the source it is possible after the knowledge has been passed to the higher mind to replace the emotions with opposite virtues such as love, compassion, tolerance and forgiveness.

Whenever the wrong emotions are aroused, when confronted by people for whom you have no sympathy or liking, deliberately bring into your mind the thought that these people also have their own problems and faults. They are evolving in the same way as you are. Are you so perfect that you can afford to judge another? Did not Jesus say, "Judge not, that ye be not judged"? Remember if these people have the power to upset you, then there are faults within you. People with bad manners, selfishness, thoughtlessness, without love are spiritual "cripples". Recognise that they have the same impulsive thought problems as you have. However, you have the advantage that you are beginning to understand the nature of the impulsive mind and have the knowledge to correct it. Apply the same two-mind analysis (sublimation) to their problems as you are already doing to yours. In other words, use the other people as your teacher. **They are an example of what you are!** In this way you will learn to offer sympathy and understanding not only to them, but to all mankind because they are mankind.

There will be times, perhaps, when you may be unable to bring control to the impulsive mind and which may result in a heated confrontation. The student should never dismiss the incident or try to forget it, but deliberately bring it back to the mind and reconsider it in every detail. This can prove to be a very painful procedure as the student would rather forget it. There is a significant reason for this. So he must carefully consider **why** he wishes to forget the incident. The answer will prove to be that he was ashamed of his failure to control the emotions. The shame is not only a stark recognition of the fault within but, in a way, is a kind of self-forgiveness.

Another very effective technique of controlling the emotions during an awkward and lengthy confrontation is to bring to mind the thought, or image, of a particular person of great quality of character and one for whom you have a great respect or love. For example, a priest may bring to mind the personality of Jesus Christ. Then ask yourself, "How would that person respond to this situation"? Or, better still, imagine that that person is actually in the room with you. This method eventually, if not immediately, develops a spiritual alertness and provides a subjective restraint. The technique must be practised again and again until it becomes a habit. Eventually, but with absolute certainty, these methods will develop within the mind a sense of self-awareness together with a power to detach yourself instinctively from the impulsive, destructive actions of the ego-mind.

The Power of Prayer

The higher spiritual reaches of the mind are God-like. Therefore, God is reachable and knowable because He is the sole object of man's highest aspirations. The first part of man's evolvement is fundamentally concerned with self-discipline. Which, as already described, is the elimination of all the faults of the lower man or ego-self. These faults are constantly reflected daily in our way of thinking, living and in our reaction to other persons' behaviour.

It is not enough simply to change our manner or behaviour, but we must consciously aspire to evolve spiritually through prayer, meditation and renunciation. The final stage of man's approach to total enlightenment – knowing God – is the Unitive Life. In other words, achieving perfect harmony through all the levels of consciousness from the highest to the lowest. The approach to this complete harmony can only be aided and accomplished by sincere prayer. There is no other way. Many people find prayer a difficult process. Start simply with vocal prayer. There are many books available containing several kinds of prayer. Find a quiet, relaxing corner and concentrate on a particular prayer. Patiently focus on the **meaning** behind the words. Imagine that you are talking to a supremely kind soul and that He is listening carefully to every word. Speak the words with feeling and with meaning. Never forget, **someone** is actually listening to your words. No prayer is ever lost. Every sincere prayer projects great power.

It is possible to offer prayer without actually using words. This is known as mental prayer. Sit quietly for a little while, think of someone on earth, in spirit or God. Send out thoughts of love. Spend a little time reflecting on the supreme wonder of the Cosmic Spirit – it is God. He **is** there – the entire universe **is** God. All of nature, humanity, birds, flowers, insects and animals **is** God. Think of the miracle of life in all these things and fill your mind with wonderment and awe. How long is it since you gave sincere thought to the miracle of life? All these things you have simply taken for granted, yet they truly are miracles. Think, where would the world be without flowers and birds?

Another type of prayer is a little more difficult because it dispenses with words and positive thought. This takes the form of meditational concentration. It is purely an intense emotional phase where we concentrate upon the truth that God is the Supreme Love, Truth, Wisdom and Beauty. Concentrate upon the fact that God is an inseparable part of you and you are inseparable from Him. Therefore, the Supreme Love, Truth, Wisdom and Beauty is **within you now!** During this prayer there is a "one-pointedness" concentration upon these aspects with the object of trying to realise, or become aware of them **within** you. In time a sense of the "Immanent Presence" of God develops.

When sitting in regular prayer never expect developments or results immediately. Many people when they have suffered much and after a long period of time pray earnestly for immediate deliverance. Some complain that their prayers are never answered in spite of their constant cries. The answer to this dilemma can be found in the story of the little seed. The seed is always placed deep in the dark earth. It is a place of loneliness and coldness. The seed is life and if we were able to hear the thoughts of the seed, we would also hear its cries of fear and despair. We with our limited wisdom would reach down and remove the seed from its place of great unhappiness. In doing so we should not realise that we are destroying not only the progress of the seed but also its life. Fortunately for the seed we do not hear its cries and so the seed is allowed to fulfil its journey through the dark, unhappy earth finally emerging into the sunshine above, a glorious bloom of colour. The truth is that God hears our prayers but in His greater wisdom **knows** that the best place for us is where we are NOW. He **knows** that at the right time our soul – the seed – will enter into the eternal sunlight above.

CHAPTER FOUR

APPLYING THE GIFT OF HEALING

It is the mark of the highest spiritual attainment to apply the gift of healing to the sick. Of course, it may be an easier way to experience the joys of the Higher Mind if one sits through hours of meditative contemplation, but it is a far greater achievement to attain enlightenment on the plane of matter, action and service. The truth is that one can never achieve **full** enlightenment until it is found and experienced on every level of consciousness.

The great masters always found their way by means of serving the suffering millions sunk in ignorance and who were frantically trying to find the way ahead. All mystics say that no one can rise to the highest unless they first start to help those on the lowest levels. It has also been said, "There are more saints in the high street than in Heaven". There is no level on which the outflow of spiritual force is not possible. No soul can live in complete isolation because when we become part of the human race we become an inseparable part of a family where each person has a sacred duty to the other. When we try to contract out of these obligations we are trying, as many do, to act against the natural ways of spiritual nature. This always involves effort, conflict and pain. It is therefore important that we strive with all our will and might to eliminate the baser elements of life not only from ourselves but also from all others who are searching and suffering. The man who carries out this duty because of love and understanding is not entangled in a world of action and **reward.** It is a conscious expression of his spiritual nature.

Unfortunately, far too many people act because they desire something for themselves. It is the "fruits" of the action which are attracting them. This truth is implicitly expressed in the words of Jesus, "The giving of a cup of cold water in **My Name** is not without its reward". In other words, for any act of spirituality to be effective it must be performed not for its own sake, but in the name of the Higher-Self. The giving of a **cup of cold water** my be expressed in many different ways; a word of hope and kindness, a smile, a gentle touch and the giving of healing to another.

Healing energy is stupendous force and perpetual. An everlasting creative power and a true expression of **inner** meaning into **outer** form not only for the benefit of the one, but for the whole of humanity. The spiritualised soul is an infinite vehicle, an innumerable network and channel of the highest intelligence which unmistakably and positively points the way to total liberation from all suffering.

To have any understanding of healing and how to apply it, we must first have a thorough understanding of illness and disease. In addition to that we must have an understanding of the nature of man. As has already been stressed many times in these pages, man is far more than just a physical body. He exists on a variety of ego-mind and spiritual-mind levels of consciousness. The body itself has nothing to do with the creation of illness; it merely **reflects** the effects of the conflict between various levels of consciousness. These different levels of mind-energy, or consciousness, are naturally and intimately linked with the physical. Many mystics conceive of these levels of consciousness as strata of varying energies between which there is a constant interplay and interaction. In the healthy person these different energy levels exist in a state of perfect harmony, but when illness or disease occurs this indicates, and is a manifestation of, a state of imbalance somewhere between the emotional, intellectual and spiritual levels.

When a healer attempts to heal a body he is actually trying to restore the state of balance. But first he must identify the area of disturbance. Next, he must eliminate the conflicting forces to provide the necessary harmonious conditions so that the patient's own in-built, self-healing process can begin to operate. It would be very unwise for the healer to leave the patient with the impression that the cure, or healing, is entirely the responsibility of the healer. No healing can ever take place without the full co-operation of the patient. When starting out to identify the area of imbalance the healer should realise that the process of disturbance is a two-way action. That is to say, it can be a psychosomatic symptom in which a prevailing emotional disturbance (worry, fear etc.) reflects directly upon the body, or a somatopsychic upset. This means, in effect, that not only is the mind capable of disrupting the normal functioning of the body by affecting certain organs, but the condition of the body (or thoughts concerning the condition of the body) can trigger off disturbing mental states. This interaction is not only capable of exacerbating the original body problem but can set up other disturbing factors.

The healer's first duty is to talk to the patient. Question the patient about any changes resulting from alterations in his emotional and physical states. It is always highly therapeutic to encourage the patient to talk freely about his life style or any worries or fears concerning new or possible changes in his environment or circumstances. It is difficult for the layman to realise that anything of an abstract nature, such as fear, jealousy, hate, resentment, worry and anger can have a detrimental influence upon the body. No more than he can accept that love, harmony and peace of mind can have a beneficent effect. This is why medical science has largely failed, because scientists are very much limited in their concept of Man, the mind, the material body, its properties and behaviour. Medical scientists, and the ordinary people they serve, need a wider conception of the **Whole Man** if they are to make any real progress concerning the ailments of man. Unfortunately, most doctors today still tend to confine their therapeutic efforts to the physical level.

But the spiritual healer must go much further than this. He must heal the **whole** man on **all** his levels. Everyone must develop this sense of "wholeness" if we are to remain whole ourselves and seek to raise our patients up to that level where the **spiritual** healing energy flows. There is nothing wrong with the material world. It is still a divine creation, but it is only when man **mis-places** himself in the material world that things go wrong. Man is essentially, and eternally a **spiritual** being but makes the serious mistake of identifying himself totally with materialism. For a time man imprisons himself **by his five senses** within a finite realm of materialism and remains grossly ignorant of the fact he is an **infinite** being. This is an unnatural state of affairs with the result that the soul and mind are seriously limited in their expression and like a flower in a dark cellar they become starved of essential energies. So disease and suffering are the obvious effects.

Of course the material world has a divine part to play in man's evolution. Just as the conditions of the deep dark earth are necessary for the development of the plant-seed, so the material world was created as an instrument to bring about first the awakening and then the development of the soul-seed within man. The plant-seed instinctively thrusts its energies ceaselessly higher and higher, through the darkness until it emerges into the light above. Likewise the soul-seed must learn to transmit its energies of a higher order upwards until it transcends the illusion of ignorance (darkness). Disease only comes when man wrongly identifies himself with the instrument, remains ignorant of the divine purpose and allows himself to become immersed in the material. Nevertheless, the experience and acquired knowledge of the darkness and its limitations serve to cultivate within man a desire for detachment and the elimination of all earth desires so that he eventually becomes free of the ceaseless rounds of pain and suffering.

What is Spiritual Healing?

If man was no more than a conglomeration of activated matter, protons, electrons, neutrons and protein which go together to make up millions of individual cells then conscious life would have no individual significance. There would be no consideration for philosophy, ethics or morality. All of man's highest aspirations would be totally pointless.

Every religion in existence teaches us that man is of an infinite **spiritual** nature which cannot be extinguished and continues even after the physical death to develop and change. All life is subject to natural law. Whilst man has the freewill to make his own decisions and to create actions within his physical and spiritual limitations he must accept the responsibility for his own actions. All actions are accompanied by emotions and many of these emotions are in effect conflicts which may also manifest as diseases. Fear is a disease; jealousy, hatred, suspicion, anger, greed and selfishness are all diseases. Spiritual healing is the greatest power of love and he who earnestly offers healing to his fellowman becomes as a living and loving God.

Long, long before the advent of man-made medicines, as far back as we can trace the history of man, there have always been special people who had the indefinable gift of healing others by the incantation of prayer, by complex rituals associated with religious beliefs, by herbal potions or by simply placing their hands upon the body. The methods known are far too numerous to be recorded here. In spite of the vast variety of techniques in most cases remarkable cures have been witnessed. Even today many strange and illogical techniques of treatment are applied and still a remarkable number of cures are recorded. The reason for this is that in all instances there was present a basic common factor – **a genuine emotional desire to heal!** This is the only qualification a healer needs, compassion for his fellowman. In other words, the **outflow** of spiritual energy. These forms of treatment are considered by medical practitioners as a direct contradiction to medical science and when confronted with evidence of obvious cures this is dismissed as suggestion, self-hypnosis and even imagination on the part of the patient. If this be the case then why is it that animals and small babies respond remarkably well to spiritual healing?

It is foolish and irresponsible for any doctor or medical scientist to simply ignore or dismiss any method which shows the slightest promise of offering relief to the suffering.

There is an abundance of scientific evidence available to prove that the healing energy is not only a real and potent force, but it is also an **intelligence** of a far higher level than our normal awareness. The writer has been subjected to a number of scientific tests which have proved conclusively these very points. For example, every sincere healer is conscious of a great heat which emanates from his hands when applying healing. Later in this chapter we will describe an experiment carried out by conventional scientists which proved beyond all doubt that the heat was not of the body but, in fact, something of far greater significance.

One remarkable case which proved conclusively that the healing force was not just an energy, was dramatically demonstrated during a visit to Vancouver, Canada. Following a talk to an audience of some 400 I asked if anyone in the assembly needed healing. To my deep concern nearly 50 people put their hands up. Explaining that owing to shortness of time I could give less than one minute healing to each person I asked the people to form a line and walk past the platform in front of me. For approximately one minute each I placed my hands on them.

As the line moved forward there came up to me a little girl aged about eight years who, I noticed, was completely without hair on her head. I automatically assumed that she had a desire to have a head of hair. I placed my hands on the top of her head and after attunement began the healing to give her hair. Six months later I returned to Vancouver. One evening I received a telephone call from the mother of the little girl. She told me that at the time I treated her daughter she already had an appointment to go into hospital to have an operation. I told the mother that I was a little confused because at the time of the healing, six months ago, I thought that the girl's only problem was lack of hair. The mother replied, "No, she had a malfunctioning kidney and the operation was to remove the kidney. But when I took her to the hospital three days after your treatment the doctors examined her and were amazed to find that the damaged kidney was completely healed". She went on to explain that the doctors could find no explanation or reason for this phenomenon. They had never before experienced such a sudden reversal with this kind of case. Needless to say, the operation was cancelled.

Another scientific experiment which actually proved to be too successful was organised by an independent television company and a teaching biologist of one of London's biggest hospitals. The biologist provided a live cancer culture which was proliferating and kept alive in a test tube. With the help of a computer they knew exactly how many live cells were contained in the tube. I was asked to apply healing energy to the cancer cells. After about ten minutes' treatment they took the culture away and when it was returned informed me that 50% of the cells were dead. Further treatment was applied once more and after another computer test it was revealed that again 50% of the cells were dead. Seven hours after the experiment it was discovered that every cell in the culture was dead. This experiment was never broadcast because it was felt that it would raise too many hopes and, secondly, I would never be able to cope with the great demand for treatment that would automatically follow.

Many potential healers, about to begin their own practice, having talked to more experienced healers and, perhaps, read a number of books on the subject, become somewhat confused regarding the right method of administering healing. If this problem should arise they should remember that every healer, no matter how knowledgeable or experienced, is solely dependent upon the one and only source of natural energy from which all healing is derived – **that source is the divine spirit within.** The emotions of love, or compassion, are involved in every act of healing and without this spiritual intervention no healing can take place.

The spiritual healer should bring to mind as often as possible the thought that body, mind and soul are indivisible and that nearly all physical disturbances are due to emotional and mental conflicts. **The body itself is incapable of creating diseases or illness.** A total understanding and acceptance of the spiritual essence of man is essential to recognising and understanding the **cause** of these problems. In other words, man's **reaction** to his physical environment and circumstances **are** the cause.

The close and interpenetrating relationship between the

physical and the spiritual bodies is gradually becoming wider knowledge so that in the very near future scientific medical research will be forced to turn its attention to this field if they are to make any further progress. The realistic healer never makes the mistake of thinking that he can do things better than the doctor or that he can replace him. The healer's sole concern should be that only through his awareness of the spiritual nature of man will he be able to restore the inner harmony and balance where there was once mental and emotional conflicts – the cause of the pain!

Types of Healing

In Britain and many parts of the Western world where healing is recognised and practised they speak of various methods, or classifications, of spirit healing. Generally they divide these into three categories. Namely,
    (1) Spiritual Contact Healing
    (2) Magnetic Healing and Radiesthetic Diagnosis
    (3) Divine Healing.

Spiritual Healing

Most spiritual healers believe that their healing techniques are directed and sometimes controlled by spirit intelligences other than their own. This belief is in evidence because spiritual healing organisations are, in nearly every case, closely associated with the Spiritualist movement. Modern Spiritualism is supported by a vast array of evidence gathered over the years by groups of psychic research scientists. Most of this evidence is extremely impressive having been painstakingly researched and recorded by groups of scientists of outstanding scholarship and integrity.

Over the years this huge mass of recorded accounts has been critically examined by the long established and internationally famous Society for Psychical Research and all the possibilities of explanations along normal or natural lines have been carefully examined and where not conclusively proven have been put aside. Therefore, the principle of the survival of the human spirit after its physical death is in no way illogical, unreasonable or to be lightly dismissed.

Furthermore, the records are innumerable where patients themselves have seen, or been conscious of the presence of personalities other than that of the healer's. Many healers, the writer included, will openly tell you that through their psychic sensitivity they have often been aware of the presence of a controlling entity. Because of this rapport many healers are automatically guided to the right part of the body and often receive "inspired" thought as to the cause of the problem. Some healers are so gifted in this way that an accurate diagnosis of the disease is instantly imparted to the mind of the healer. Most sensitive people, including healers, are able to project help to patients without touching them or even being in their presence. This is achieved by a process of prayer and meditation and is referred to as Absent or Distant Healing. However, this technique will be dealt with more fully in the next chapter.

Interested people frequently ask what sort of physical conditions will respond to spiritual healing. Providing it is not a problem created before birth, or a genetic one, it is reasonable to say that every condition at one time or another has responded to spiritual healing, but it would be an untruth to say that **every** condition has responded **every** time to spiritual healing. Among the successes associated with spiritual healing are the dispersal of tumours and cancerous growths. Though there have been many instances where an immediate change has been witnessed, normally treatment is a slow process during which the swellings and pains are gradually dispersed. The remarkable thing is there is never any visible dispersal of the tumour. Obviously, some internal body factors are aroused which clear away the foreign matter. Healers should never expect this to happen every time, perhaps many healers will never experience it, but it has certainly come within the experience of a great number of healers.

Goitres, curvatures of the spine, prolapsed discs within the spine, stomach ulcers and various forms of arthritis are amongst the many problems which may benefit fairly quickly from healing. Curvatures can be straightened within minutes by an **experienced** healer. Every possible type of disorder can respond to treatment but the healer should leave the timing to the healing intelligence. Many cases can respond quickly, even when complicated, whilst others which may be considered simple will require many treatments. It is generally accepted that all healers work under the control of a "spirit" helper or guide. Some healers are conscious of this, but should the healer not be conscious of this presence then do not be dismayed because without doubt your helper is there working alongside you. Given sufficient time his or her presence will be felt.

Magnetic Healing

There are many healers who do not consider themselves to be **spiritual** healers. The magnetic healer believes that stored within his body there are energising forces. These forces are transmitted to the patient by a series of passes which are made through the aura of the patient. The aura has been subjected to many scientific tests and it is the opinion of many of these scientists that the aura is an electrical energy field intimately associated with the body and actually forms a link between the physical body and the mental body. This electrical field is widely accepted by conventional scientists because it can be detected and measured by instruments. Many researchers believe that an aura is a radiation of the energy from within the billions of cells which make up the human body. Considerable evidence is available concerning this human electrical field but it is not the purpose of this book to provide such details. Clairvoyants have often witnessed this phenomenon and described it as composed of scintillating lines of light surrounding and interpenetrating the body. Some say there are actually two auras interpenetrating each other. One extends for about three cms and the other about 8 – 10 cms.

Some clairvoyants are able to see the aura in colour which,

they say, rapidly changes with the emotions of the person. The late and extremely gifted healer and clairvoyant, Ronald Beesley, was not only able to describe changes which took place within this field in accord with changes in emotional and mental activities, but he was able to sketch the auric pattern of his patients complete with colours. In addition to this remarkable feat he would describe not only any current illnesses but relate to past illnesses and accidents which, he said, always left their impression behind.

The passes made by the magnetic healer, which are used to stimulate and soothe, are said to generally conform to the laws of magnetism as understood by physicists. In other words, the hands of the healer may be compared with that of a magnet passing over a magnetised or non-magnetised piece of metal. The energy-depleted areas will be sensed and so attract the magnetic energy of the healer.

Magnetic healers tell us they are very much different to the spiritual healer. Whereas the spiritual healer depends upon the power emanating from a deep spiritual source within himself or from the spiritual helpers around him, the magnetic healer does not rely upon any such spiritual source for his power. He believes that the energy is created and stored within his own body and that it automatically radiates towards and re-energises the depleted areas of the patient's body. This means that the healer will experience a depletion of energy, in which case he must wait for a time until the power is regenerated before passing to another patient. Many spiritual healers do not agree with this division but believe that all healing originates from the same source. Personally, I believe that all healers have a common source. Therefore, it would be difficult to leave aside the spiritual aspect.

Radiesthetic Diagnosis

Certain healers may at some time be questioned about this technique, therefore a few words on the subject would not go amiss. The healer or diagnostician involved in this technique uses a pendulum which can be a very simple affair. Usually a piece of string with a small object made of glass or plastic tied to the end. The pendulum is used as a kind of divining agent to pinpoint the troubled centres of the body. The patient is asked to lie down on a table or couch and the pendulum is suspended above the body. First, the healer "mentally" tells the pendulum to indicate whether anti-clockwise is "yes", or clockwise is "no", or vice versa. The diagnostician believes by analysing the movements of the pendulum he can tell whether the area is healthy or sick. This method has been used for divining many objects or conditions, such as whether a particular food is good or bad for a certain person. For many years it has been used by dowsers to find water, oil, old pipes hidden in the earth, mineral deposits etc. With the use of a map it has even been used to locate missing persons.

Divine Healing

In this form of healing the patient is led to believe that his sickness is the direct result of many sins he has committed. To achieve perfect health the patient must have a total and absolute belief in Almighty God. God is perfect and therefore created everything perfectly. Sickness is a manifestation of imperfection, lack of faith in God. Therefore as man himself is capable of the creation of that which is imperfect he is also capable of eliminating the imperfect. This can only be achieved by renouncing his sins and giving all thoughts to God and Jesus Christ.

The divine healer believes that his healing is brought about by the **direct** intervention of Jesus Christ. The treatment consists of the laying-on of hands and the continuous incantation of prayers which are sometimes followed by anointing with oils. Should it follow that the patient does not make any recovery then the inference is that God is not yet ready to forgive him. This pattern of treatment will be repeated many times and should it continue to fail then it could have an adverse psychological effect upon the patient. Throughout this form of treatment the patient is being led to have faith in God and Jesus Christ.

With spiritual healing the patient is not questioned as to whether he has faith or not or whether he has a religion or not. The only qualification required of a patient is that he has a sickness and is prepared to follow the advice of the healer should he feel that a change of life style or way of thinking is necessary to sustain the cure.

However, let us not look disapprovingly on divine healers. They are sincere and dedicated people and they do achieve wonderful results. However, we must make note of the patient's frame of mind and ask ourselves whether a series of failures could not arouse a deep feeling of guilt which may have a serious psychological effect upon the patient. Spiritual healing should be simple. Devoid of rituals, creeds and dogmas. The patient should be made to feel "at home", allowed to relax and not be disturbed by questions concerning his faith, religion or beliefs.

The Old Testament awes us with its description of the miraculous six-day creation of nature. This is a gross mis-interpretation of the words of God. Creation was not a series of physical acts but the perpetual movement of eternity. Such thoughts were in the mind of Edward Carpenter ("The Art of Creation") when he wrote, "Creation is a stupendous renewed work of art, an everlasting evolution and expression of inner meanings into outer form, not only in the great whole, but in every tiniest part. Nature is a great vehicle, an innumerable network and channel of intelligence and emotion. The in-telligences which constitute the universe are doubtless of infinite variety and of infinite graduation in development . . ."

The countless millions of species of insects, birds and animals represent inventive ingenuity of the highest order. Though man is considered to be the highest order of individualised spiritual expression we are still physically and spiritually an inescapable part of the infinite variety of intelligences. Human beings are not only totally dependent upon one another but are inexorably bound to every other form of life. We are all held within the same Spirit or Divine Mind which is individualised in the tiny microbes as well as the highest creative achievement – Man!

Disease common to **all** life. A sustained state of disorder or disease either in the human form or in any of the species inevitably precipitates a slow decline and once a particular life form fails to contribute to the process of progress it could be the beginning of its extinction from life. The records of natural history are replete with information concerning the life of now extinct species which once shared this life with us. Now all we have to remind us of their active lives is a collection of fossilised bones.

Disturbing change in environmental conditions and natural resources, very often brought about by man's greed, set in motion the process of devolution. Unfortunately, this phase of environmental destruction and extinction of species has not been halted. In fact, we note it has been accelerated as we continue to observe the obvious and slow disappearance of other forms of plant and animal life. Man is as yet unaware that we are not only dependent upon one another but also very much dependent on every other form of life, Man is a **spiritual** being and no less a part of nature than the tranquil trees and flowers and yet he still manages to live in daily conflict with the entire world of nature. All forms of vegetation, when allowed to grow naturally, free from the damaging interferences associated with man's artificial cultivation methods, remain healthy and wholesome. This is because there are no conflicting emotions associated with these beautiful elements of nature, even though they are as much a natural living organism as is man who depends upon the same vital spiritual life force.

Medical science remains totally oblivious of the "whole" nature of man and the **cause** of disease and prefers to continue to concentrate on the **physical** manifestations of what are actually **inner** disorders. They are fascinated by the many descriptions and diagnoses of the multifarious malfunctions, but fail to realise that in reality they are all similar, meaning that they are expressions of the **same** thing – **conflict between mind and soul.** This state of ignorance is the one and only reason why modern medical science has failed to cope with the basic disorders which inevitably involve decay and disease.

Before we can possibly achieve a state of disease-free living we, as individuals, and medical scientists, must set out to understand the **whole** of nature. If patient and scientist fail to achieve this understanding then man, too, will become extinct. In short, the approach and the solution must, ultimately, be spiritual. Conventional medicine which relies so heavily upon artificial drugs will provide no other benefit than a temporary cessation of a particular group of symptoms, while the cause which remains undetected will ultimately give rise to further manifestations of spiritual imbalance.

Healing Techniques:

When considering the widely different techniques used in the application of spiritual healing it is of vital importance that we discover if there are different values in the various methods employed by different healers. Also to assess whether there are factors common to all methods. Methods vary from the Christian ceremony of the anointing of holy oils; the African witch doctor's frenzied dance rituals and his application of noxious concoctions to the victim's body; the blood-splattering operations of the Filipino "surgeons"; the simple laying-on of hands, to deep-trance psychic operations where the healer's hands will perform in intricate detail a complete mime, with invisible scalpels and other surgical instruments, comparable to physical operations.

Other unusual techniques which have been observed include placing the widest end of an aluminium trumpet over the patient's affected area. Then the healer violently blows the healing "energy" down from the small end. Other healers have been observed using small wax dolls which are placed over the diseased part of the body during which prayers for help are offered. The dolls are then placed in a sanctuary, or chapel, where it is believed they will eventually draw the pain from the patient's body. The "combing" of the aura by the healer's hands is a fairly common technique particularly in Britain. The belief is that inner disturbances pass disharmonious effects into the aura which can be "combed" away by the healer's hands.

Many potential healers are naturally confused by the incompatible differences between respective healers. However, despite the differences and the symbolism underlying each technique it does appear that in a majority of cases much benefit is imparted to the patient. Each of the healers believes that they are spiritually interpreting a ritual which is the best way to convey the power to remove pain and restore health. The basic common factor involved in **all** methods, no matter how bizarre, is **compassion** – a sincere spiritual desire to help a fellow man. The technique in itself is not important, but has simply acted as the **stimulus** that opened the channel for the flow of spiritual energy. The spiritual healer, the orthodox priest and the jungle witch doctor are united by the **same** spiritual power which, stimulated by their desire to heal, flows to the aid of the patient. Compassion, the highest form of prayer, answers all calls for healing. It is no respecter of religion, belief or personality.

In healing **by the spirit**, the brotherhood of man is a reality. The spiritual healer by his method, presence or kindness of personality will nearly always provide a stimulus that creates a reaction within the patient. The reaction could be entirely psychological, which is beneficial or there could be a direct positive reaction from the spiritual force of power transmitted by the healer.

The most common form of healing is that of the laying-on of hands. The healer places his hands above or on the affected part of the body and then proceeds to attune himself to the spiritual source within. There are a number of ways of achieving this. All are effective because, remember, it is the **desire** to heal that evokes the healing energy. First commence by turning the mind inwards. Bring to mind the following thoughts. The physical body has no spiritual power whatsoever. The mind and soul are infinite sources of divine power. Now concentrate upon the fact that this unlimited healing energy already lies within you. Use a prayer or the image of a holy man to help the attunement. Then mentally project it either through the entire body or through the hands to the patient. After the lapse of one or two minutes both the patient and the healer will be conscious of heat emanating from the hands.

This healing-heat has been tested and recorded by scientists. Furthermore it was discovered that the emanating heat is also of an intelligence which is greater than that of the healer's. This was discovered during a test when a group of scientists suggested an experiment to discover if the heat was, in fact, simply an accumulation of normal body heat. A set of electrodes were attached to the hands of the healer. A patient, provided by the scientists, was seated in a chair. The healer then began to attune himself which is the time when the heat begins to generate. After several minutes the recording machine failed to respond. After checking the instruments the healer applied himself once more. Again, the machine did not respond. After some discussion the "patient" disclosed that she did not suffer from any ailment, but was, in fact, perfectly healthy. Afterwards another person, with a physical problem, was found and placed in the chair. Within seconds the machine began to record the heat waves and the patient described a power flowing through him. The startling conclusion which arose from this experiment was that though the healer was totally ignorant of the fact that the first patient was healthy, the healing intelligence imm- ediately **recognised** the fact just as it recognised the presence of a disease in the second person. Furthermore, the scientists reported that it was not an accumulation of body heat because the machine recorded a heat **much higher** than the normal body temperature.

This experiment has been tried several times with a mixture of healthy and sick patients and every time the healing intelligence has succeeded in distinguishing between the sick and the healthy. Therefore, it is useful for potential healers to know that it is not necessary to have the gift of psychic diagnosis or to know where the physical problem lies in the body. The healing intelligence will unerringly find it.

All healers with whom I have come into contact agree that the healing power and intelligence are derived from God. Even though the healer, the priest-healer and the witch-doctor will proclaim that their powers are divinely inspired the priest will, very often, describe the healer's and the witch-doctor's powers as being of satanic origin. The healer should not be disturbed by this. He **knows** that he is appealing to a divine power and only a divine power can bring about relief from disease and suffering. The priest is simply postulating theological dogma. God does not have a religion nor does He overburden Himself with creeds and dogmas. God sees only humanity.

If we are doing our best to help one another, even if unknowingly doing it the wrong way, it is still a spiritual act, therefore an act of healing which is divine. There is a piece of advice which all healers should keep in mind, **"It matters not what others think of you, but it is very important what you think of you"**.

Some healers ask the question whether it is necessary to prepare themselves before attempting to give healing. Healers of various church denominations and beliefs do have particular rituals of preparation such as fasting, hours of meditation and prayer. Though I do not think it is necessary to fast or spend several hours in meditation or prayer, it would be beneficial to give a few moments to silent prayer. Having spent the day in an office, shop or factory during which it is necessary to work in association with the intellect or ego-mind, the healer must now attune himself to the inner healing intelligence. To achieve this he must subordinate his own personality to a higher concept of service. In other words, the individual must give way to a "one-ness" with humanity. A state of spiritual integration must take place to allow him to tune-in to a source of power that is totally within himself.

Whilst the various methods used are open to a wide interpretation and discussion I believe that **simplicity** is the perfect answer to effective healing. Healing, no matter how spectacular, is not a miracle. All cures are achieved within spiritual and natural laws. If the patient persists in breaking one of the laws then he must suffer the consequences. Therefore, the healer's first task is to discover where the patient has gone wrong and persuade him to change his ways. No healer is sufficiently powerful to bring about relief if the patient stubbornly refuses to change certain ways. Healing is the stimulation of natural, or spiritual, processes. Both healer and patient should strive to create a spiritual influence so that a state of balance is achieved. Disease can only exist where there is a state of imbalance – healing is spiritual as well as a mental process.

Where the healer is confronted with a painful, twisted or stiffened limb after attuning himself he should use gentle physical actions to free the limb. This is sometimes called "manipulation" which is not strictly true. Once the healer is mentally attuned he is actually working with the natural healing flow, or rhythm. He should be so in tune with this flow that he can painlessly straighten out a twisted limb or ease out the osteo-adhesions which are preventing the movement of the limb.

It may be necessary to apply the treatment several times throughout the week before it is free or straight. There is no doubt that these manipulatory movements are extremely valuable providing the healer "feels" for the limits of the limb's movement and does not attempt to go beyond these. Each treatment will extend the limits of the limb until it is finally free. It is an old-fashioned idea to believe that a healer should just rest his hands on the part and not attempt to manipulate the part. Very often the use of physical action is of considerable benefit. But, I repeat, "feel" for the limitations and do not go beyond this.

Not all patients come to a healer with a physical problem. Very often there is a mental disturbance. In this case it is not sufficient to simply lay hands upon them. I always say that a good healer is a good listener and a good speaker. Every sensitive healer is equipped with an inner voice of intuition. After some experience this will become obvious to you. Always commence by allowing the patient to talk uninterrupted. This in itself is highly therapeutic. After listening patiently for as long as is necessary, your inner voice of intuition will provide you with positive clues as to how to respond. You will be able to attune

95

yourself to the difficulties within the patient, sense the difficulties which are creating the inner conflict or putting up barriers which are preventing the action of the patient's own inner healing forces.

Never draw back from attending to a mentally disturbed patient. Within every healer there is an inner spiritual knowledge which will unfailingly provide the right words and give confidence to the patient and restore them to a happier frame of mind. Remember, with all patients, and mental patients in particular, you **never** work alone. The healer should not hesitate because he feels he is not a psychologist or psycho-analyst. By guiding the patient to the source of his difficulties the inner spiritual knowledge, or voice of intuition, will reveal the correct information and not only help you share the patient's burdens but will considerably relieve the mind of the patient. Every healer, with experience, will eventually develop his own way of healing. The power of intuition will gradually grow and the healer will eventually have in his possession an extremely powerful therapeutic tool.

Healers should keep in mind that all healing is a two-way venture. Every patient possesses an inner self-healing system and if the healer works without attunement then the healing is only mental, therefore sterile and empty. We must care deeply, completely and intensely. **Feeling** is the fuel behind every healing act and love generates the healing fire.

When we pray our thinking should create the awareness that we and the patient are an inseparable part of the divine universe. During each moment when the patient is lifted into the ideal spiritual atmosphere the patient's system of self-healing begins to operate. All healings take place according to divine law and as health is a state of spiritual balance the rapport which the healer must create will bring about great benefits. We need this sense of "Oneness" if we ourselves are to remain healthy and we need this sense of "Oneness" if we are to lift the patient up and away from the inhibitions which are creating the conflicts. Disease only comes when we forget this, when we lose sight of the fact that we are a holistic (body, soul, mind) being and become immersed in the trough of materiality and illusion. This is a direct reversal of all the natural and spiritual laws which only means one thing – chaos and conflict.

It would help the healer considerably if he would spend a few minutes every day contemplating the following truths:-

If God created the earth and all living creatures in it then the origin of life **must** be spiritual.

All life is part of God. It has an infinite spiritual nature which is not changed after the physical death, but continues to develop towards finer levels of consciousness.

The physical body is in a state of constant changes. It is the **outside** world of man. It is the sole duty of the mind to maintain a state of balance and harmony.

Experience in the material world is both physical and spiritual. Physical experiences and reactions are unreal and impermanent and only affect the physical. All spiritual actions are real and permanent and add to the development.

Good health is a state of spiritual and physical harmony.

The spirit or deeper mind which healthily nourishes the soul is the thought of God.

All life is subject to natural and spiritual law. Whilst these laws allow freedom of thought and action within our physical and spiritual limits, wrong actions and reactions within this pattern must ultimately be paid for.

Every soul is subject to the laws of cause and effect.

Spiritual healing is the greatest power of love. It brings peace to the patient and progress to the healer.

Anger, fear, greed, hate, jealousy are diseases of the mind which eventually manifest in the body.

It will not be until spiritual power is recognised by medical scientists and all people will the world be free of disease and chaos.

We experience effects which others have sown, we are free to sow causes which will affect others.

Some Healing Experiences

I am frequently asked the question, "What kind of diseases respond to healing?" It would be true to say that every disease has responded to spiritual healing at one time or another, but it would be untrue to state that every disease has responded every time. Spiritual healing is not the direct intervention of God in which natural and spiritual laws are broken. All healings take place **within** the boundaries of these laws. Spiritual healing is simply an attempt to restore the original state of harmony disrupted by conflicts in the relationship between body, soul and mind. Therefore, spiritual healing needs the close co-operation of the afflicted person.

The action of healing is exactly the same, and as logical, as those of the therapist who works to heal the body by physical means. The healer must be a sensible and responsible person at all times. He must in no way create the idea that he can replace the orthodox medical practitioner. Many medical therapists are healers in their own right by unconsciously imparting spiritual healing through their understanding and consultations with patients. The simplest way to answer the question, "What kind of diseases respond to healing?" would be to draw upon the records of actual cases.

The first case concerns a young man who arrived from Switzerland, "I have just been to see my doctors after tests informed me that I have a serious tumour in my testicles. The hormone count is very high, whereas in a healthy person it is much lower. They want to operate immediately to remove the tumour as it could develop rapidly. Instead, I choose to be treated by you". For five days I gave the patient treatment lasting up to 15 minutes. He then returned to the hospital where he underwent further tests. "The doctors were amazed" reported the patient, "the hormone count had returned to normal. They could not believe this and insisted that I undergo a surgical operation to make sure that the tumour had in fact gone. I knew that the tumour had gone and that there was no need for an operation. As they insisted on this, I agreed. The result was they found no signs of the tumour".

The next case took place in the Philippines, the home of the psychic "surgeons" who open bodies with the fingers resulting in the release of a lot of blood. The patient was a lady who had had a goitre for some eleven years. Orthodox surgeons and psychic "surgeons" had made several attempts to remove the problem but without success. After my usual attunement I took the goitre between my fingers and gradually it grew smaller and smaller until it was no more. The immediate and puzzled reaction of the Filipinos present was, "But where is the blood?" Many months later I received a letter from the lady informing me that the goitre had not reappeared as it did when treated by the others.

The next case took place at a large public meeting in Basle at which were present a large number of doctors. A young girl came forward with a chronic curvature of the spine. The spine was shaped like the letter "S". She had had hospital treatment but, again, without any sustained effect. After being examined by a doctor, I concentrated for about ten minutes on the spine during which the girl remarked that the heat was rather uncomfortable. Then slowly I straightened the spine which became perfectly straight. The same doctor immediately came forward and again examined the spine after which he declared to the audience, "What he has done we cannot do in the hospital". I gave a similar healing to another young lady in Perth, Australia. She already had an appointment to have an operation for the straightening of the spine. Once again the spine became straight. A doctor seated in the front row came forward and asked if he could examine the spine. Afterwards he asked the girl, "Did you feel any pain?" Upon telling him that she felt nothing he turned to me and said, "For us to do this in hospital we must first anaesthetize the spine, therefore this healing power must also be able to anaesthetize bones".

The next case fulfilled a most cherished hope of mine that some day doctors and healers will work together. A surgeon working in a hospital brought a boy of about ten years to me. The boy had fitted to his face a moulded plastic mask. On removing the mask the sight was horrific. Areas of erupting flesh covered the boy's face. The mask was to prevent the flesh from further proliferation. It appears that the boy's face had been badly burnt. The surgeon had skilfully grafted skin from other parts of the boy's body. For several months it was healing perfectly then suddenly it begun to break out and proliferate. I detected that there was some unknown element within the skin's pigmentation which when cut began to multiply. I suggested to the surgeon that I should give spiritual healing to the boy for two months in order to inactivate the unknown element. Then it would be safe to "shave-off" the surplus flesh. This we did, then several months later the "shaving-off" operations began. Today the boy has an attractive face showing a few scars which, I am sure, will disappear in time.

Epilepsy is an illness which responds readily to spiritual healing. There are too many cases to record in this chapter, but there are two most notable ones which are worthy of a report. The first was a little girl of about nine who for seven years suffered fits and blackouts every day, sometimes several in one day. After one treatment she had no further attacks. The second case was a man of about 25. Ever since birth he suffered attacks nearly every hour of the day and night. Every form of medication had been tried but without sustained success. He received treatment from me once a week for about two months and gradually the attacks became less and less. The severity of the attacks was also greatly reduced. Today, he experiences an occasional attack, but being an extremely sensitive man I suspect that emotionally he is not yet in full control, and when he himself achieves this there should be no further problems. The list of cases is endless. There are others concerning blindness, asthma, arthritis, anorexia nervosa, deafness, dermatitis – all these and many others have responded to healing. Nearly all results achieved through spiritual healing are progressive. Very often only one treatment is sufficient, but there are times when the treatment must be given over a period of time. Regarding this delay I feel that the fault lies with the patient. Very often they are holding on to a way of life which is detrimental to the body. Other times, I suspect, the patient enjoys the attention and "service" they receive when loved ones are over-caring.

There is still much to learn about healing even though we will never know the true nature of the healing energy. All we know is that it is a force of the spirit, therefore its source is spiritual and it will only come into effect for its beneficent work when there is complete spiritual rapport between the healer and those who are not totally wedded to a material way of life. For the potential healer there are no set rules; no training is necessary. There is no school on earth which can teach the soul to radiate love, compassion and tolerance the only channels accepted by the Healing Intelligence. There is only one rule I would submit to my readers, "The cause of all disease is **self** and the state of **separateness** from our spiritual being".

The Healing of Animals

The power of spiritual healing it not confined to human life. All life including animal, insect and vegetation is an inseparable part of the Divine Spirit. Therefore all life, in whatever form, can be influenced by healing power. Animals have the same God as humans and therefore react to the same power of love. The law of love and compassion makes no difference between humans and animals or any other form of life. There never can be one law for animals and another for humans because there is only **one** God – the Creator of all life including the microbe and vegetation. There are no such people as "specialist" healers. There is not one kind of healing for humans and another for animals. Though every healer is also an animal healer the healer must extend the same love to them as he does to humans.

Animals are our brothers and sisters and they are entitled to the same respect, consideration, care and dignity as our brothers and sisters. During the years I have devoted to healing I have been instrumental in treating all kinds of animals, including cats, dogs, birds, horses, tortoises and even pet rats and mice. Animals and babies respond in a remarkable way to healing which clearly eliminates the old-fashioned belief that to receive full benefit from healing one must have complete faith or have a religion. Even a belief in God is not necessary. There are many kindly, even saintly people, who **intellectually** reject the idea of a living God, but have much love, compassion and thought in their heart for other people and animals. The only qualification a person, or animal, needs to receive healing is an illness or problem.

There was a time when I received a telephone call from an extremely distressed lady. It was Sunday morning, I was in Zurich and I was to fly back to London within a few hours. The lady was concerned about her horse which was in an animal hospital. The veterinary surgeon had informed her that the animal had a serious infection in the stomach and nothing could be done except to shoot it. I hastily went to the animal hospital and placed my hands, first, on the horse's stomach but I was then drawn to the chest. I asked the doctor if he had placed a tube down the horse's mouth. He said he had. I then asked him if by accident the tube had gone into the lungs. He said that was so. I then told him that the lungs were also infected. However, after about 30 minutes' healing I left the hospital. One week later I was told that the horse was back with its owner. One year later I learned that the horse was alive and still very active.

There was another time when my own pet cat, "Nelson", was saved from the vet's impatient lethal needle. I had returned from a trip to the Continent when my wife anxiously informed me that "Nelson" had not eaten or drunk water for three days. He was totally inactive and showed no interest in life. We took him to the veterinary clinic and the verdict was that his kidneys had collapsed. As he was seventeen years (exceptionally old for a cat) the vet was of the opinion that nothing could be done and the kindest thing we could do would be to have him put to sleep. All my instincts told me that he was wrong. I told the vet that I would take the cat home and would bring him back in three days.

I have always been of the opinion that no person or animal is too old to have healing. I commenced healing immediately. Three days later I took him back to the animal clinic a completely different cat. Though we cannot of course make anyone younger as age is a natural process, he was alert and his coat was once more "alive" and healthy. Once more he was eating and drinking and occasionally romping around the garden. That was nearly one year ago, he is still with us and approaching his eighteenth birthday.

The technique for treating animals is exactly the same as for human beings. Place your hand on them, attune yourself through prayer, then concentrate on your hands imagining that the energy is flowing outwards. Should you have a collection of animals in your healing room awaiting treatment then it would be wise to take precautions regarding spreading infection to other animals. Always have available a bowl of water containing disinfectant to wash down the table or floor where the animal has rested.

Animals of all types respond very readily to absent or distant healing and there is plenty of evidence to suggest that animals are more receptive to this form of healing than human beings. It is not even necessary to know the animal. As long as you have a name or photo one can project distant healing, and it is surprising how readily they respond. When treating an animal never be afraid that they will harm you. It is really surprising how docile and gentle animals become when they are being treated. Some sixth sense tells them that you are there to help them. The healing energy somehow seems to induce a deep relaxation.

It is generally believed that animals are much more psychically receptive than humans. When brought to a clinic regularly they seem to know when it is time to leave for treatment and even when it is approaching the time for distant healing (their owners tell me) they usually settle down and relax at the right time. Birds also seem to know when someone is trying to help them and will calmly settle down in your hands when healing commences. This not only applies to pets or household birds but also to wild birds. On countless occasions I have been led to an injured wild bird. I have taken them home, treated them, and after a while they have happily flown away. There was one occasion when my wife told me that a pigeon often walked into our garden. She said she believed it had a broken wing. I sent many thoughts out to that bird. Then early one morning I heard a tapping at the window and when I turned to look there was the pigeon with the broken wing. I walked out into the garden and he remained quite still on the window-sill and I was able to pick him up. I realised immediately that I needed the skill of a veterinary surgeon to set the wing. This was eventually done and later the bird was released.

It is not always the right thing, simply because an animal is getting on in years, to simply put him to sleep. Just like aged people animals can live out a happy, if not too active, life. Even in old age animals can suffer a temporary infection or distress, but given the right kind of conditions will recover from that problem and go on to live out a few extra years. Old age is never sufficient reason to put an animal to sleep. Most animals can achieve a higher degree of relaxation than humans. Animals when feeling "off-colour" will naturally seek out certain plants and herbs which are therapeutically beneficial to them. Keep the thought in mind that most animals have a very well developed recuperative power and will frequently overcome the most appalling injuries and conditions without much assistance from their owners.

CHAPTER FIVE

ABSENT OR DISTANT HEALING

In all of my seminars which are organised all over the world I have always been impressed to state, "Thought force is the only creative force in existence". I know this to be true because, when we think about it, every created object in the world is the result of thought.

Mystics accord to the mind (the source of thought-power) the superb power to manipulate thought symbols which when applied to the world give us the achievements of all things pertaining to natural science. Mystics also accord to the mind the functions of feelings, emotions, imagination through which we are able to bring forth in tangible form inspired music, art and the language of poetry and words.

There is another function of mind which is, perhaps, some still higher level of Self, and that is the mystical intuition which is able to discern infallible knowledge which we know as **truth.** The greatest spiritual teachers of mankind have always had perfectly developed higher minds and were capable of re-markable acts of healing from a distance. The function of the higher level of mind is to express spirituality of a high order . . . namely, both contact and distant (or absent) healing. A famous Irish poet and mystic said, "Words would often rush swiftly from some hidden depths of consciousness and be fashioned by an art with which the normal brain had but little to do". Mystics also say that there are two distinct levels of mind. The one level is that which senses only the world around us and the other links our vital centre of consciousness to a higher world including the spiritual-etheric world. One mystic suggests that in some cases the mind sinks towards the infinite "unconscious" and then on to the (Buddic) highest level of spiritual consciousness.

From the above the reader should begin to realise that thoughts directed from the highest levels of consciousness have absolutely no concept of time or space therefore, in no way, can be confined by them.

This level of consciousness is infinite, therefore is the "one-universal-consciousness" uniting all mankind and living things. It is difficult for the ordinary man to get away from the thought that he is a limited being functioning in a particular place when in fact he is an infinite being with a infinite level of consciousness capable of embracing everyone and everything. It is for this reason that in the earlier parts of this book I stressed the need for regular prayer and meditation. Only on these levels of spiritual consciousness will we be able to practise contact healing and transmit healing thoughts through the universal consciousness to the sick. It works very much like a radio, only much more accurately without interferences. With radio technique there must be the transmitter (healer), and the receiver (the patient).

The desire to give absent healing requires the same qualities of higher consciousness as contact healing. In other words, all who inwardly "feel" for those who suffer possess the healing potential.

Requests for absent or distance healing are usually made directly by the sick person, or an intermediary – a friend or a relative. It is not essential that the sick person should be informed that they are receiving healing over a distance. In fact a number of experiments have been carried out to see if there is any difference in the power of the healing when transmitted to a person who requests it directly or to another person who is unaware that they are receiving healing. The records showed that there was no appreciable difference in the results. In the latter case it proved beyond doubt that the element of auto-suggestion played no part in the healing. This point was further proved by the fact that very young babies and animals respond extremely well to distant healing.

It is unfortunate, but a number of people think of absent healing as the "second-best" method. It may be that these people think of it as more abstract and less tangible than contact healing, therefore it is not so realistic. This is a completely false idea. Distant or absent healing is an extremely potent force. It is very real and equally as effective as personal contact healing.

The best proof I can offer is to relate two factual instances.

One evening I received a telephone call at my home. The caller was a lady owner of a small dog. Full of anxiety and fear she informed me that her little dog had not eaten food for four days and had stopped drinking water three days previously. I did now know the lady nor her dog. I told her I would commence distant healing immediately. This I did. The next afternoon the same lady called again over the telephone. She sounded excited and happy and then proceeded to tell me that when she arose the following morning the first thing she noticed was that the food bowl was empty and the dog was busy drinking water. Early afternoon, the veterinary surgeon arrived at the home to put the dog to sleep as he had promised to do the previous day. She told him that she had already taken the dog for a long walk, and that he had eaten a good meal and was quite active. The vet could offer no explanation for this "miraculous" cure and left a very confused man.

There is another remarkable distant healing story involving Pope John Paul II. The incident occurred during the year 1962. According to a top journalist, John Paul II, then Polish Bishop Wojtyla, was on official church business in Rome when he received news of a close family friend, Wanda Poltawska, who was close to death with cancer of the throat. Doctors had declared the cancer incurable and inoperable. They told the woman to prepare herself for dying.

The future Pope's thoughts immediately went to Padre Pio, who had been accredited with hundreds of miraculous healings. Upon contacting him, John Paul II begged the monk to give distant healing through prayer to this friend. Padre Pio, who has since died, (in 1968) and is now being considered for Sainthood, responded and prayed for the health of John Paul's friend. Within a few days a joyful John Paul informed the monk that his friend had been instantly and completely cured of cancer. This had been confirmed by doctors. Wanda Poltawska was a married woman of 46, the mother of four children. When the padre received John Paul's letter he was living in a very small convent in a Southern Italian town. He himself, old, and a very sick man was rapidly going blind. The letter was read to him by Angelo Battisti, the chief administrator of the small local hospital which the monk had helped to build.

Padre Pio told Battisti, "I cannot ignore this, but keep this letter because one day it will be very important". "Then the Padre", says Battisti, "immediately withdrew to his tiny, austere cell and began to pray for the woman". Several days later another letter arrived from Bishop Wojtyla. Battisti then read the letter to the padre. "Venerable father, the woman from Krakow, the mother of four children, was instantly healed, just before the operation which the doctors had later decided to attempt. Thanks to God and thanks to you too, venerable father on behalf of the woman, her husband and all her family".

Bernardino da Siena, Head of the Vatican Commission considering Padre Pio for Sainthood, confirmed, "The testimony of Pope John Paul II in his letters is a solid fact. Father Domenico Mondrone, Editor of the Jesuit magazine Catholic Civilisation, said, "I've had those letters from Pope John Paul II in my possession. They are most certainly authentic and include testimony that he witnessed a miracle through the prayers of Padre Pio".

Absent healing can be more advanced than contact healing because these prayers create a **direct intercession** through spiritual attunement with the higher level consciousness of the healer and the patient. As absent healing becomes more and more practised with understanding and dedication this method, in time, will assume ascendency over all other methods of healing. Furthermore, it is an established fact that those people who have the inner desire to help the sick and wish to develop the power of contact healing, can adopt no better method than absent healing to arouse this latent power. Even though the transmission of the healing force has not taken place by direct contact and the patient has not been touched or even seen by the healer the mechanics of this form of healing is such that the sick person actually receives a healing stimulus of sufficient strength to **set into motion** the natural self-healing system within the patient. In many cases the patients are totally unaware that healing for them has been asked. In many instances they are in a state of mental turmoil and, very often, sceptical. Which proves that there can be **spiritual acceptance** of the healing force without physical conscious acceptance.

Many times the question has been put to me, "If you do not know, see or contact the patient, but the sick person gets well just the same, why is it necessary to contact a healer?" The healer is a transmission agent. The spiritual influence requires a material link so that it can manifest upon a physical plane. Though the patient may not make the request, a friend or relative would provide the necessary link. Therefore, via the friend or relative a spiritual-physical link is formed which permits a direct contact to be made. There are even many records available when a sick person has simply desired healing from a particular healer and a healing has actually taken place before the physical communication has been sent.

Over the years a number of surveys have been made by a number of associations including the Spiritualist Association of Great Britain and The Harry Edwards Sanctuary to assess how successful absent healing, or distant healing, really is. It was discovered that the results achieved were extremely positive. The average percentage of successes were between 60 per cent to 80 per cent. During my work as General Secretary of The Spiritualist Association of Great Britain I have had the opportunity to meet and talk with many doctors and I was surprised to learn that many of them actually submit names of their patients to absent healers. Many of these doctors stated that they were very surprised to see how these patients benefited from the absent healing and many times surgical operations had to be put off.

There is so very little we know about the power of distant healing and yet its effects are so awesome and beyond understanding. Some years ago a German television company made a feature-length film about my healing work. App-roximately fourteen patients were selected to take part in a documentary about healing. Each patient had a long medical history of a particular physical problem and each patient had been told by their doctor that nothing more could be done medically. For a period of nine to ten long weekends I treated each patient which was filmed. When the TV film was broadcast it created a nationwide interest. The remarkable interesting point was that many people watching the programme and the healing techniques had similar physical problems to those in the film and many of these sufferers suddenly found their own problems disappearing. **They were being healed by tele-vision!** This was obviously another form of distant healing which was not only new to me but came as a great surprise. In some inexplicable and mysterious way the healing power being demonstrated on TV was creating a distant rapport with the viewers. Coincidence? Auto-suggestion? Maybe, but many of the viewers, I was later told, were sceptical unbelievers and were not impressed at all until their own problems began to disappear.

There was another mysterious example of absent healing which happened over the radio in Australia. It was during a "talk-back" show (Where the public and the radio controller talk with each other via radio and home telephone). A lady came onto the line and she asked me, "Can you tell me what my problems are?" Immediately I replied, "Yes, you have a serious painful condition starting at the back of the neck, extending down the spine and affecting your knees".

With a voice showing obvious amazement she said, "Yes, that is absolutely correct". Then I told her, "Do exactly what I tell you to do". I then instructed her to stand up and relax completely. I told her that after a few minutes she would feel a very warm sensation starting at the neck which would move down the spine and into her legs. I then said to her that when she felt this warmth in her legs she was to slowly bend down and touch her toes. At first she was afraid to do this because it was something she had been unable to do for some years. Finally,

112

she did it. There was a gasp of amazement followed by a loud cry, "I've touched my toes!"

Auto-suggestion you may think but the very next day this theory was destroyed completely. I was in my hotel room when the telephone rang. It was a lady whom I did not know. She was very excited. She said, "I was listening to you on the radio and the diagnosis you gave that lady fitted me exactly. I had the same pains from the head down to my legs. I listened carefully to the instructions you gave that lady and I followed them out myself exactly to the letter. Within a few minutes all my pains disappeared; I was touching my toes and today I feel like a nineteen year old girl'.

There is no way I can explain that phenomenon. The healing intelligence is infinite. Wherever the thought is, or the desire, to receive healing it immediately reaches out and makes contact. It does help considerably if the patient is able to 'tune-in" with you at an appointed time. It also helps if you have a photograph of the patient in front of you. Nevertheless, if neither of these arangements are possible distant healing will still work as it does in the case of babies and animals.

Some healers have such a large list of patients that it is not possible to make an individual direct mental link every time. This can prove upsetting for the healer because he feels that as these people are relying upon him he should be treating each one personally. The healer should not be disturbed by this situation. He can use a general intercession procedure. He should type out a complete list of his patients complete with a brief description of the problem. Take, for example, twelve names. Concentrate upon the names and the problem. Then send out a single prayer to cover those twelve. Then, take another twelve and do the same thing again until the entire list is dealt with. I can assure the reader that the healing will be just as powerful.

There is just one exception. Should the healer have one or two patients who are critically ill, then these patients should be given a special concentration. Frequently it has been said to me by many of my patients that during the absent healing session they have actually seen me in their room. Many other healers have reported the same phenomenon.

There are many people who "feel" that they can heal, but are not confident enough to try. Or, perhaps, they have not got the opportunities to practise. In that case there is no better way to arouse the latent healing powers than by the absent healing method. Furthermore, it will greatly assist the facility of attunement that is so necessary for contact healing. No other method assists the beginner more to bring about that vital rapport with the spirit realm.

For nearly twenty-five years I have practised, not only contact healing, but absent healing. This has entailed many hundreds of hours of meditation and attunement. And I have proved beyond doubt that there does exist this mental faculty of transmission of thought first from the healer to the healing intelligence and then from the intelligence back to the healer and to the patient – indeed, every act of absent healing has proved this to be so. The **only** required condition for healership is that there should exist a state of spiritual attunement between the healer and the intelligence. Always bring to mind the fact that you, and every human being, is a **spiritual** being and by spending fifteen to twenty minutes on spiritual things, or prayer, you can create a spiritual rapport.

The question of how long we should concentrate upon each patient is one which is often asked. First, the healer should never clutter up his mind with pleas to God to help the patient because these are just wishful thoughts. Wishful thoughts do not heal. Only complete attunement with the Higher Intelligence heals. All healing is simple. The Healing Intelligence has a greater vision and awareness than the healer and is capable of coming into action as quick as a thought. After attunement, or a feeling of "Oneness" with the inner self, the Healing Intelligence automatically and instantly creates a rapport between healer and patient, as soon as the healer directs a thought to Mrs X who has a tumour (or whatever the problem).

There is no need for a long concentration of thought. When this happens all you are doing is filling your mind with your own thoughts. This can be tiring and time wasting. Once the attunement has been achieved the healing act between healer and Healing Intelligence begins. I cannot stress enough that **attunement** with your inner spiritual being is the vital secret of successful healing whether it is distant or contact healing. At first the healer may feel completely inadequate, but with practise and experience he will quickly learn to achieve a smooth almost instantaneous rapport. Sit in a place where you know you will not be disturbed. If possible always use the same room because an atmosphere of power gradually builds up and remains there for some time. Also it will help the build-up of atmosphere to have in the room a cross, crucifix, a painting of Jesus Christ, a saint or some other holy figure. Keep the room simply furnished with a few fresh flowers and, if possible, a plain altar to hold the photographs of patients who cannot visit you.

It would be ideal if it were possible to set a small room aside to be used solely for meditation and healing. There is no need for patients to travel to such distant places as Lourdes because the same spirit, the same spiritual rapport can be created in your own little room. It is as one great spiritual teacher said, "A cathedral can be created wherever you sit or stand". Remember, the Absolute Spirit and Creator is already within you and it is simply a question of attunement and then you are ready to reach out with your own spiritual power to heal. Where there is sincerity there is instant rapport with spirit.

All healing is governed by spiritual law. No healing can take place outside of these laws. Thought of God **is** spiritual law in action. Every change that takes place within the universe is decreed by this law and there are no exception to it. Many priests believe that when they pray to God, in response to their pleas, God will over-ride His established laws. This is wrong, the approach is wrong and is the reason why so many prayers appear to remain unanswered. No one, no patient, who repeatedly goes against these laws can receive much benefit from healing. It is possible, and it has been proved, that with repeated distant healing (even without them knowing) the patient's way of thinking and living can be gradually changed.

I remember a man who lived in the apartment above me who was a habitual drunkard. He was aggressive and extremely unsociable. I commenced distant healing for him. Within a few weeks he completely changed his ways, gave up drinking and we became the best of friends. All this was accomplished without even talking to him. Always remember that it is the patient's attitude of mind which allows the Healing Intelligence to reach him, or it can create a barrier.

The healer should not be upset or worried if on some evening he forgets, or is prevented from carrying out his distant healing intercessions. The Healing Intelligence will not forget. Many times a distraught relative or friend has approached me and pleaded with me to give distant healing to a sick one. I have patiently listened to the details of the sickness and made a mental note to include them on my list and promised to send out healing. But there have been times when because of an over-busy schedule and many things to think about I have forgotten my promise. Yet, surprisingly, the relative or friend has contacted me and thanked me profusely for the wonderful healing as the patient had made a marvellous recovery.

The answer to this lies in the fact that whilst I was listening to the problem of their friend I **sincerely** desired and meant to project healing to that person. The **sincere desire** emanated directly from the inner spirit and made the necessary connection. This is a very common experience and if one talks to a number of healers they will tell you the same story. Whenever the healing thought is sincere and purposeful it will unfailingly create the required rapport. Never be casual or impatient when directing the healing thought, because you will be wasting your time. At the same time do not linger too long with your own thoughts over your patient or continue to implore the Healing Intelligence to take special notice of your patient. Sincerity and dedication instantly make the connections.

When a healer is receiving requests every day from new patients with the result the list gets longer and longer it is not necessary to repeat the distant healing procedure every day for all the patients. The Healing Intelligence already **knows** and

116

does not need reminders. It is far better to devote your extra time to meditation in order that you may improve your method of attunement. Of course, we do not entirely forget our old patients. Occasionally go back to them. Of course there are always those patients who are critically ill and need our particular attention.

Even when it is known that a certain patient has died or is about to die the healer should not be distressed or hold the thought that he has failed. The healing has not failed. In fact the healing has most probably been of tremendous benefit to him. No one dies by accident or bad luck. Every movement in the universe no matter how mundane or complex has already been decreed by spiritual law. Every living thing is subject to constant change. Just as leaves on the tree "die" only to be re-born again so the human being undergoes a physical "death" only to be re-born again – **in spirit**. This transformation (which is part of life and cannot be avoided) can be a beautiful or difficult experience. The application of healing, be it contact or distant, is always of tremendous help to those who are about to undertake this transformation – or re-birth.

It is a well established fact that those people with a terminal cancer and who have received regular healing do experience a painless, calm release. A few years ago I had an elder brother who throughout his entire life was obsessed with the fear of illness and more so with the fear of dying. One day this brother's wife telephoned me to tell me that the doctor had told her that my brother had a terminal cancer in the stomach. He did not know this but believed it to be indigestion. Because of the distance between our homes it was only possible to give him one treatment of contact healing. From then on he received distant healing.

One evening they were sitting together, he did not feel ill nor was he in pain, when he turned to his wife and calmly said to her, "Sybil, I hope you will not mind when I have to leave you, soon". One morning, a few days later, his wife arose from her bed to see to the breakfast. My brother sat up in bed and called for his wife to join him. She later said, "He was very calm and

117

relaxed and then he said to me, "It is time to go now, goodbye, and thank you for everything" then he lay down again and within minutes was still". This, to the family, was a most astonishing incident knowing how terribly afraid he was of dying.

There was another incident concerning a man who had a great fear of hospitals. He developed a serious stomach problem and the doctors were quite confident that a surgical operation would put everything right. But the man stubbornly refused to consider going into hospital. His wife asked me to put him onto my distant healing list. This I did. One week later the wife came to see me looking very happy. Then she told me the story. Her husband, she said, had awakened in the middle of the night and quietly said to her that he no longer had any fear of going into hospital therefore she could make immediate arrangements for him to have the operation. He had the operation which was a complete success. Very often it is necessary for patients to go into hospital and have an operation. Again this is not an indication that spiritual healing has failed. When a patient is due to go into the hospital for an operation it is always very beneficial if the patient receives spiritual healing before the day.

It is common knowledge among healers that whenever healing is administered prior to an operation the recovery rate is much more rapid than when no healing has been given. There will be many times when spiritual healing and surgery work successfully together.

The way of Attunement

There are several ways of seeking attunement with spirit but each way is a form of quiet meditation. One should always adopt the most comfortable way and this could mean sitting in a chair or on the floor, but never in bed. Bed is suggestive of rest and sleep. Never meditate feeling hungry or after a heavy meal. The clothing should be loose so that the healer has a feeling of freedom. Meditation should take place in the dark or in dimmed light. Very soft, gentle music may be played.

118

Sit quietly for a few moments gently breathing in and out until you establish and become conscious of a rhythm. Now turn the mind "inward" and concentrate upon the thought that you are the Eternal Spirit NOW. Further, the absolute power of the spirit, the absolute wisdom and beauty of the spirit is actually lying dormant within you NOW. Continue to concentrate on the thought that THIS is actually you. This spirit within you has all the powers necessary to heal. Then quietly abandon yourself to this inner you. You cannot force it to operate, only your awareness of the spirit will enable it to flow outward. You will experience many interruptions by the surface-mind thrushing in mundane thoughts. Never become irritated by this but quietly bring back the thought of awareness. Never forget the meditation **and** the interruptions are part of the meditation. No one can meditate too long on the spiritual awareness. With practise you will be able to extend the time of the awareness.

If there are not too many patients on your list, or if you wish to give special treatment to someone who is seriously ill then you can use the "image" method. This method can only be used on someone you know personally. Because it entails visualising the sick person. Create a clear picture of the patient but create a healthy picture.

First, they are smiling quite happily at you. They look healthy and wholesome. Then visualise them engaged in some healthy activity such as jogging, swimming, playing with the children, singing and dancing or anything else you can create. In other words think of them being very healthy. If they are very ill and are confined to their bed visualise the bedroom (if you are familiar with it). Walk over to the bed and place your hands on the body and go through the same procedure as if you were giving them contact healing.

We have mentioned many times the need to meditate if we are taking up a life of healing. Jesus said, "You should pray continuously". By this he meant that we should never stop meditating. Meditation does not begin and end in the meditation room, but should occupy the best part of our day. This is not so impractical or difficult as it may seem. Healing is a spiritual venture. Though the body needs material things to sustain it, such as food, clothing and entertainment once these duties are performed we should bring the mind back as often as possible to the fact that we are essentially a spiritual being. Healing can only be accomplished by the spiritual being. Therefore we must weave into our daily life a code of true spiritual values.

The surface mind is impulsive and reacts almost without thinking. It can reflect anger, frustration, impatience and even dislike of someone. These are unspiritual reactions and the very opposite to the healing thoughts. We said earlier in this book that we have among us physical cripples, who have been unfortunate to be born with an imperfect body. To these we give love, help and tolerance automatically. But there are also the spiritual cripples who live, act and think in an unspiritual way because of their lack of progression. We, the wiser ones, who are more spiritually aware are the only ones who can help their progression **by our example.** Anger breeds anger, hate breeds hate. Love, gentleness and tolerance provide the antidote to hate and anger. If you, the healer, cannot provide this then who else can? It is solely up to the more spiritually aware to help the less spiritual. As Jesus said, "If your brother strikes you on the cheek, offer him the other".

Therefore to "pray continuously" we must be tolerant and generous to all no matter what they do to us. We must avoid doing harm to anyone, but only seek to serve them. We must not allow bad temper, ill will or thoughts of revenge to be the reaction to another person's action. When faced with a difficult or irritating situation ask yourself the following questions. "What part of me is hurt, pride, dignity or ego? If I retaliate what do I actually gain, self-satisfaction, a new stature or power?" Always check the impulsive mind first, then think before reacting. Help your neighbours and friends in every way you can. If you see a sick or crippled person in the street make a mental note and add them to your distant healing list. Always remember, your difficult neighbour is your best teacher because the karmic laws have selected him to reveal the weaknesses within yourself.

No healer should take upon himself a promise to bring about a cure. This raises false hopes and will later reflect upon the healer's competence. Many times I am asked how many treatments will be needed before they are cured. I always reply that as I am only the vehicle I cannot answer that question nor can I promise a cure. That is the responsibility of the Healing Intelligence.

Most healers will at some time be asked the question by a patient as to whether they should cancel an impending surgical operation. Again the healer should never take upon himself this responsibility. I usually reply that if the operation can be delayed (with the doctor's permission) I will apply the healing for as long as possible and then ask the doctor to make a further examination in the hope that sufficient progress has been made to delay the operation further or cancel it altogether.

Healers should not concern themselves with diagnoses. Some highly sensitive healers can do this but it is not necessary. Diagnosis is not healing. The Healing Intelligence will recognise the problem and where the problem lies immediately. To attempt to diagnose can be dangerous and misleading especially if the healer leads the patient on to have more confidence in him than in the doctor.

All absent healing entails a certain amount of correspondence. Remember each letter is a vital link between you and the patient. Each letter is a report from the patient and the reply should always be "natural" as if the healer was actually talking to the patient. Read the letters carefully and try to "sense" the mood of the patient.

Later when you commence the distant healing sessions have the letters beside you in the healing sanctuary. Encourage your patients to write to you. Remember, they are expressing themselves to you. This can be a tremendous relief to them, therefore, therapeutic.

No healer should place himself in a position where he can be blamed for the deterioration of a patient's condition. There are those patients who place too much reliance upon the healer and will not go to see a doctor. Many people are afraid to see a doctor in case it is really bad news and they may have to face an operation. The healer must always co-operate with the doctor and advise the patient to see a doctor first. This advice in no way reflects a lack of confidence in the healing, but it will save the healer from a lot of trouble should the condition deteriorate and even lead to the death of the patient. This way does not mean that the healer lacks confidence but that he is showing some common sense.

It has often been said that contact and absent healing is purely psychological or a question of auto-suggestion. It is very true that both of these suggestions play a very important part in healing. Both can be very therapeutic. When a person writes to you for distant healing they are feeling distressful, anxious and depressed. To know that someone is thinking of them and sending out prayers for their improvement can be psychological. When they write back and report that they feel an inner-upliftment, an added vitality and strength, this means that positive feelings have replaced the negative ones – this is highly therapeutic. It would be quite safe for the healer to say in his reply to them that they can expect an upliftment and a new feeling of vitality. For a patient to be encouraged to look forward to a better time and better feelings is psychological but it can also be extremely therapeutic. However, be cautious in your letters, do not deliberately raise false hopes. Do not make promises.

Many people are overjoyed at the knowledge that they have the power to heal and so they set out with the thought that they can with this power cure everyone. Unfortunately, they will meet with many disappointments. They will not be able to do this. There will be times when they will be instrumental in curing a very difficult case and at other times a simple condition will refuse to respond to the healing. This will create disappointment and even the thought that the healing power is unreliable and only works for some.

What the healer must realise is that with the difficult case the **cause** may not be difficult to remove. With the simple condition the cause may be very deep seated. Every condition manifesting in the body is telling us that there is something wrong in the thinking, the living or in the mental emotions of the patient. The patient may be holding on to the **cause.** Do not forget that every illness **must** have a cause. It is simple, at times, for the doctor, or healer, to remove the effects but if the cause is still existing it will reflect in a different way in a different place at a later date.

A good healer always searches for the cause. Therefore, the success of a healing depends as much upon the patient as it does the healer. To help the patient to realise this important point I always use the illustration of the boiling water. If a person insists on putting their hand into a pail of boiling water which will produce an extremely painful condition, the doctor, or healer, is able to remove these conditions given sufficient time. The hand will remain healthy as long as the patient keeps his hand out of the boiling water. Unfortunately, he has the free will to do with his hand whatever he wishes – even to putting it back into the boiling water. In other words, if we do not change our ways of living and thinking we cannot enjoy an uninterrupted healthy life.

Some healers will experience embarrassment when a patient offers them a free-will donation. Should they accept it? There are a number of factors which must be considered here. First of all the patient wishes to express their gratitude and they can do it in the only way they can, by offering a donation. To refuse this is denying them this little pleasure. It might even hurt them. Then, of course, there are the healer's expenses. The buying of writing paper, envelopes and stamps. Buying little things to enhance the sanctuary, etc. I therefore suggest that there is nothing wrong in the healer accepting free-will donations sent to him in gratitude.

In conclusion it is hoped that the chapters dealing with contact and absent healing will not only be a means of helping sick people, but (as it is the purpose of this book) help the reader to achieve an awareness of his own substantial inner powers. To open the way to a fuller understanding of the spiritual potential within and so advance not only the health, happiness and

progress of his fellowman, but to awaken his own deeper, inner
consciousness that he may realise that his is Spirit NOW with an
eternity of spiritual progression ahead of him.

"Truth, perfect health lies always within
ourselves. It pays no heed, whatsoever
to outward things.
Whatever the beliefs of those around you,
know that there is an undying innermost
centre within all of us. There truth
lies in all its fullness simply concealed
by a wall of flesh".

Tom Johanson